THE SIXTH SOLA

It Is Time to Move On from the Past 500
Years of *Reformation*, to the Next
500 Years of *Transformation*

MICHAEL WARD

Copyright © 2020 by Michael Ward.

All rights reserved. This book or any portion thereof may not be reproduced or used in any manner whatsoever without the express written permission of the publisher except for the use of brief quotations in a book review.

Publishing Services provided by Paper Raven Books

Printed in the United States of America

First Printing, 2020

Paperback ISBN = 978-1-7347312-0-0
Hardback ISBN = 978-1-7347312-1-7

TABLE OF CONTENTS

Chapter 1: Introduction — 1

Chapter 2: The Discontent — 17

Chapter 3: The Great Relationship — 37

Chapter 4: In the Beginning Was the Holy Spirit: The Book of Acts Chapters 1–5 — 47

Chapter 5: Saul to Paul to Philip to Peter, Acts 6–10 — 55

Chapter 6: The VIQ: "Did You Receive the Holy Spirit When You Believed?": Acts 11–19 — 75

Chapter 7: Still in Jail after All These Years, Acts 19–28 — 99

Chapter 8: Sola Spiritu Ambulatio — 115

Chapter 9: Luther Leads With Reformation: I Lead With Transformation — 141

Chapter 10: The Plan and Call to Action — 171

Chapter 11: Transform the World, One Person at a Time — 193

CHAPTER 1
INTRODUCTION

Welcome to the *Sixth Sola*! It's been quite a journey to arrive at putting these thoughts on paper. Some say ideas need to marinate before being released into the world. And that's what has been happening. This journey started on December 13, 2013. The last few years, I have asked many questions about hope, faith, and love. Perhaps you have as well.

Before going any further, let me introduce the title of this book, and why I call this the Sixth Sola. In theological circles, there are the Five Solas. They developed from the Protestant Reformation, mainly Martin Luther. Now I don't want to lose anyone here, right from the start, so let me assure you, this is not an academic book. You did not pick up a theoretical book about Christian doctrine. This book will resonate with those Christians who have a sense of commitment and consistency to continue to be faithful to their particular church. It doesn't matter where you are coming from, it only matters where the Lord takes you next. So be assured, though I will sometimes use theological terms, this book is for those who would say they are "Christian" or are curious about Christianity and who believe the forms presented may be lacking in power and purpose.

Now, back to the Solas. Recently, the 500th anniversary of the 95 Theses, which Martin Luther nailed to the Wittenberg door in 1517, was celebrated around the world. Not just Lutherans, but nearly all Protestant churches acknowledged the people and events from half a millennium ago. This was not the pivotal moment of faith for Martin, but more of his rant against the practices of the Christian church at that time. He would live his life in pursuit of understanding God the next 40 years. And during those years, he would have many experiences that would form the foundations of what we now call the Reformation. Certainly, there were others involved during these years of change. And I mention this not to debate the nuances of who is responsible for what, but to point out there was a time that we may have thought is insignificant today but may actually be continuing under the surface.

A brief summary of the Five Solas:

The Five Solas:

1. ***Sola Scriptura*** ("Scripture alone"): The Bible alone is our highest authority.

2. ***Sola Fide*** ("faith alone"): We are saved through faith alone in Jesus Christ.

3. ***Sola Gratia*** ("grace alone"): We are saved by the grace of God alone.

4. ***Solus Christus*** ("Christ alone"): Jesus Christ alone is our Lord, Savior, and King.

5. ***Soli Deo Gloria*** ("to the glory of God alone"): We live for the glory of God alone.

They developed from working out a struggle with the organization, hierarchy, and leadership of the only church of that period. History is very complex and again, there are dynamics at play in politics, science, technology that likely influenced what was happening, and I wish to point out the resulting impacts that some took with regards to a faith that had established itself in some form the previous 1,500 years.

Out of these days and years of thoughts, Martin Luther came to his two foundational principles, which were: Sola Scriptura, by the Word alone, and Sola Fide, by faith alone. The remaining were also developed during the early years of the Reformation. These Five Solas have remained as foundational principles for many Protestant/Reformed organizations.

Another Sola?

Why am I proposing another? Well, it's a result of my wrestling with hope, faith, and love. Throughout this book, I weave in parts of my personal story, but more importantly, I will communicate what have I been thinking about, what am I learning, and why it should be important to you. I created my own reading program focusing on the post-Resurrection writings. If you have read this far, you will either identify with the Christian faith, or be interested in considering another's comments on what he is witnessing. And when I use the term, "post-Resurrection" writings, it's a subset of what Christians refer to as the New Testament, focusing on what took place after the Resurrection.

My fire, if you will, is on moving from the transmission of information into living the message. Religion can be a complex subject, and yet with Christianity, the events are quite peculiar. This is not a book to prove anything, or in Christian jargon, this is not an apologetics book, but more of a "let's step back" and see what the overall message is here. Is it possible we have been thinking about facts, knowledge, and missing the larger message? That's the type of questioning I wish to have you consider as we move forward.

Many Reformed churches and even Roman Catholics will have a reading from a particular Scripture, but do we consider the context, the author's experiences, what was happening at the time? This is not a scholarly review because my opinion is these are the words of God himself, somehow recorded through others. The words should not be so complex that it would take a highly educated person to decipher the meaning. One of my conclusions will be that I believe we are making this faith more complicated than it needs to be, and it might be because people continually insert themselves between the message and the intended listeners.

What I have found is that the larger context of the actual words, the timing of when events happen, the characteristics of the people to whom these words are written, and more, lead to an understanding that we may be missing because we assume these are simply the "words of God," dispensed for our consumption.

Our lives take on such complexity that this type of communication often decreases the actual power of the written word and, in the worst cases, does not fit the context. Below, I will provide an excellent example from a great discourse from Paul in 1 Corinthians 13.

Naming The Sixth Sola

To eliminate the suspense, the Sixth Sola is walking in the Holy Spirit Alone, or Sola Spiritu Ambulatio. This is not something I made up one day. Back in December 2013, I started to record and grapple with many years of Christian experiences, teachings, leaders, and personalities. I have moved from the Midwest, to the Southwest, to Germany, and back to the Southwest. I have participated in several Christian organizations, churches, and taken up leadership roles, all the while desiring to make this faith an integrating factor of my being. And one fateful day, as I started journaling, I developed what I eventually came to call the Spiritu Ambulatio. It now represents the purpose of the Holy Spirit and our calling to simply walk in the Holy Spirit each moment of every day. Others have written well about being in the presence of God, or even speak of God's providence, but why do we not call the experience and come to terms with what this power of the Holy Spirit is, that the Scriptures describe?

The Holy Spirit is often mentioned in Christianity as the third person of the Trinity, and yet it is not easy to find well-articulated explanations about how we, as followers of Christian teachings, are to engage with the Holy Spirit or allow the Holy Spirit to engage with us. My purpose here is to increase the frequency and use of what God has described for us, the Holy

Spirit, and with the frequency, increase our acknowledgement of God's power and presence wherever we are in every moment.

Since the Reformation, so many Christian churches have formed and continue to form. Many of these are due to splits, or arguments over social, political views, and cultural challenges. As a person born and raised in the United States of America, the denominations are in the multiple tens, if not hundreds. As an American culture, we have created "mainline denominations," "evangelical," "local/community/independent" organizations that all claim to represent the Christian faith.

My efforts to understand what has happened and what is taking place in our churches lead me to believe we are stuck. It's as if we are in a continual denominational reformation, which began 500 years ago and is continuing to this day. I suggest we would all benefit from acknowledging we have been in a state of reformation long enough and begin to look toward our own personal transformation.

And it starts with me. I am choosing to consider my moment-by-moment living as a walk with the Holy Spirit. It is about being in His presence. This presence enables God to do what He promised, to lead me in a better way of living, thinking, communicating, and interacting with others starting with those closest to me, in my family, neighborhood, work relationships, and this new experience we have with online communities. And I have come to appreciate that what matters is only for me to "get better," or to "improve." It's not about meeting some minimal standard and pleasing religious leaders. That's the beauty of having the mindset that God is with us at every moment. And why do we know this, if not because He often says that the Holy Spirit is with us. Perhaps, we have somehow missed what has been there the whole time.

I know many of my shortcomings and difficulties transforming, but perhaps God is not interested in improving my performance based on religious leaders' scales. Is it enough to recognize His presence in every moment? This promise is expressed in the Scriptures, yet its practice has rarely been demonstrated. It's difficult to display and appears to have less importance than arguing over correct doctrinal beliefs.

A Living Transformation

My transformation began when God intervened in my life. We all have our unique childhoods. To briefly summarize mine, I was the distant youngest of four siblings of a Roman Catholic father who had issues with his church because my Presbyterian mother wanted to compromise by raising the children Lutheran. That worked for my mother, but my father was still on shaky ground. I did the eighth-grade confirmation and for several emotional and family stresses, I simply did not have a heart-changing experience. I understood the facts of what we commonly call the gospel; they were plainly explained to me. At 14, I'd lost interest in participating in the church.

At the age of 16, my first job at a grocery store introduced me to the world of work and expanded my experience with people from various backgrounds. A person came across my path who explained that her attitude toward others changed because she understood that what I thought were just intellectual, knowledge points, were actually true. God did send His Son to allow us to have a relationship with him. And that it was through this mysterious Holy Spirit that led to one being born again. For me, that was the moment of moving from an intellectual understanding of facts to a spiritual heart taking its first steps in faith, in forgiveness, hope in this life, and, though not conscious at the time, a journey of transformation.

Perhaps I didn't fully understand this at the time, but it does not appear to me that simply preaching the gospel with the intention of changing other people has been effective. It was not my experience to be presented knowledge, but perhaps for my complex situation at home, the turmoil, this may have prevented me from connecting the message to real life. However, I now believe it is always God reaching out to us. Some may argue that the intent of preaching the gospel is not to change other people, but if one is honest and listens to many of today's messages from religious leaders, it's not that much of a stretch to get that impression. So, while technically that is not the case, practically, that is the message often sent.

After 40 years of attempting to follow the Reformed Christian teachings, I sense that leaders do often believe that they can influence change with their words or words from Scripture. But are influencing others and being the instruments of transforming others what leaders are called to do?

And each Sunday, millions attend local gatherings and hear a 20- to 40-minute message from a leader who has been called to invest hours in preparation. I have believed for too long that this weekly event was the key to spiritual practice. Yet I have come to recognize how essential an investment of my own is to bring about transformation. I likely have put too much emphasis on these weekly gatherings and not enough on my own practice.

Moving Beyond Reformation

I invite you to join me in considering how to move beyond reforming our organizations and people by prioritizing personal spiritual transformation. Some critics may suggest that this is a "selfish view." Where does it say that the faith is about "personal transformation"? My answer is that we agree that we are not all gifted in the same way, and as we progress with this consideration, the "personal" aspect is just that: We are all different. It is not making ourselves out to be God, but rather allowing the amazing people that God made us to be, to live and serve as He intends.

As a person of faith, called to love others and to maintain hope in challenging situations, what matters is walking each day in the presence of God with His Holy Spirit. I believe this has been the message the entire time, but we seem to stumble on ourselves in mostly debating who is in charge, who has the loudest voice, and separating ourselves over what might truly be trivial matters.

I choose to frame the last 500 years of Reformation and propose to move to the next 500 years of transformation, by embracing the Sixth Sola, Sola Spiritu Ambulatio. And this may be where the elusive "revival" will come from. My impression is that revival is thought of a group that is outwardly harmonious in appearance. But what if it is actually when each of us takes responsibility to walk in the Spirit and change our communications with each other. Instead of setting out a goal to achieve, let's set up systems and frameworks that encourage each other to turn toward the Spirit of the living God. My suggestion here, or call to action, is for us each to pursue our transformation. The Spirit may move and bring out gifts that He wishes to manifest in our daily interactions. It will be a movement of the Spirit that brings revival.

We are asked to renew our minds as Paul describes in Romans 12. We know these passages, but are we shown a reasonable "How"? Even before a how, we may want to ask for a why. The short answer on the why would be to have this impact on the people around us because we have confidence in God's love for all people, and ourselves. Tall order. We may never achieve this, but what about moving in that direction? And to move in that direction, what are possible hows?

My how, well, after so many years of hearing message after message, and book after book, and study after study, I thought, "Is it possible to simply read what was happening and then understand what the Living God may be saying to me?" I also asked myself, "Do I have to consider every message from other people and incorporate their vision in my life?" "Is it possible that what is working for others will never be effective for my situation?"

It became clear that, yes God can speak through the scriptures to my situation, and no, others' visions may not be for me. At the same time, I can cheer on others who are doing what they are called to do. And my solution was to invest the time in giving an overview of what took place after the resurrection. It began as a large task, and I don't mean reading the Bible in a year. I decided to focus on "our time." We live in the time of post-resurrected Jesus. He's been crucified, has risen from the dead, and ascended.

Introduction

A Chapter A Day

And I decided to read those books or letters because that's where we are now. We have the Holy Spirit; what does that mean? That question was foundational to my pursuit. I eventually added nearly the entire New Testament to my reading list. And instead of reading them in the order presented, I thought it would be important to see if there was a trend in the message Paul and others were sending based on the roughly chronological order of the texts. I added Acts as an overview and that set the stage for my how. I read one chapter a day, and I consider how the Holy Spirit may be influencing me. And that's what this book is about. It's about my experience of learning to walk in the Holy Spirit.

While reading a chapter a day from the New Testament will not guarantee that we will walk in the Spirit, it appears we don't often discuss the Holy Spirit. All of the faith communities I have participated in over 40 years have a deep respect for the scriptures and I am writing to them, asking that we take a fresh look. Look for evidence of the Holy Spirt working and ask questions about your life now. Here is a preview of what I will be describing in detail.

My how is not only to consider what took place after the Resurrection but to look at what happened next. I wanted to put these writings in roughly the order they were written and begin reading them as a rollout of what was happening. By doing this, many events took on a significance I hadn't appreciated from isolated readings. Connecting the flow brought about some variations on previous views.

My intended audience are believers, those with faith. My desire is to generate interest in what has been there the whole time. I'm not presenting anything new, but I am framing the focus not on simply learning facts and gaining knowledge about what God is doing through the early leadership.

And by early leadership, I'm referring to Peter, James, John, Philip, Saul who becomes Paul, Luke, Barnabas, the traditional names we all know, but are there personality differences, opinion differences that one should consider when reading their letters or books?

The traditional evangelical view is that this is the inerrant Word of God. I agree with that view, and I will likely repeat that statement again. However, that doesn't mean that the individual writer may not have his own life experience that influences his writing. I will point this out when we read John's description of the relationship between Jesus and Peter. There's no way Peter would record what John does for us. Peter would be embarrassed, so he wouldn't write it. That doesn't mean Peter is "errant" because he wouldn't record the events the way John does; it's just a different view and we may see how our own transformation may be similar to John's or Peter's, which are different.

Reading this way is no longer viewing the Bible as a manual of verses to be plucked out for special occasions. It's an ongoing story of God's working and the way it is revealed through the lives of his followers and soon-to-be followers. It brings context to the events and raises interesting questions.

Creating Your Own Devotional

Most importantly, though, this is not a teaching. I'm not here as a scholar, researching what took place. I have the opinion that the Word of God would not be with us if it was so complicated to understand. My recommendation is that you create your own devotional. You have challenges and relationships about which only you and God know the details.

I am showing how to use these early journeys to think about what's happening in the life of those chosen to launch this new movement. Is there an event, an instruction, a person, or a difficulty that may resonate with you on a given day? This is a daily process to follow and doing so brings strength and encouragement to your day.

I have come to see a parallel between this work and my use of a personal trainer at a local gym. After a few sessions, it became clear I didn't know what to do when I entered a gym. There were so many choices. So, for 30 minutes, a trainer walked me through how to do five to seven exercises.

The trainer didn't lift any of the weights. I had to do it myself. I now think of the gym a bit like the Bible. There are 66 books, is it best to start at number 1? Also, am I going to do the lifting each day? Or am I going to rely on someone to speak to me once a week for the encouragement, direction, and strength to face the challenges of my life? Or connect with an excellent speaker and podcast to bring motivation to my life?

We can do that, get outside motivation. But I am suggesting that we do the lifting. It's all there for us to take hold of and if we do, the transformation has the best opportunity to take hold. If it is us lifting the weights, our muscles, spiritual muscles will grow.

Another downside from the weekly pattern is that often, we may need to hear a different word from God, so why not get it all in a regular routine that you control? Take charge, be intentional in your reading.

What would it look like to get the big picture from God by "working out"? It is from a system, a routine, that I noticed the importance of the Holy Spirit and how I was missing the confidence God wants us to have in His presence.

The True Guide

Are you ready to go here about a challenge and hopefully take it on?

It is the Holy Spirit that is the true Guide. I am just pointing you to the Guide; I'm a coach directing you to the Powerful Coach. I wish to inspire you to consider what God is calling you to do. What is your purpose? It's a popular question and not just among people of faith. Yet is it something we must truly determine on our own? I ask that you challenge yourself to get the big picture of the message, take ownership over your consumption of spiritual literature, and don't focus only on one or two verses but read in large chunks to seek the big picture here. God is calling us to walk in His Spirit, so let's encourage each other on this path.

It would be bold for anyone to suggest they can guide you to your purpose, but could the Holy Spirit be calling you to a unique mission? As you read these words, you represent a miracle of creation: You breathe, you have thoughts, you have challenges, and you've chosen to invest in something that I hope will increase the amount of transformation happening in your life.

If you have in your soul a desire to serve and a gift that hasn't been fully expressed, could it be because you are waiting for others to suggest what you do? Or perhaps you believe you have to choose among existing options. But what if your calling is completely new and isn't yet widely acknowledged?

Here's a question for each of us: Am I missing a transformation that impacts my thoughts, my mind, my relationships, and am I confident that I am participating in a relationship with God, or is this relationship even possible?

If that is a question you wish to explore further, then you have picked up the right book. Let's get started.

CHAPTER 2

THE DISCONTENT

A friend from my local church gave me a box of inspirational cards called "The Resolution for Men." His hope was that it might be a form of encouragement and a means for growth. They were a set of 40 cards with a verse on one side and an intentional behavior on the flip side. There are periods in our lives when we sense our deepest emotions, we become reflective, and perhaps we have anxiety about the future.

During that time, I was faced with challenges and I saw them as a challenge to overcome. I was being called to something new. It wasn't an overnight change but a process that began and continues over several years. Transformation has become a daily walk. A step-by-step into the future. Sometimes these steps are small, sometimes they seem to be setbacks, and sometimes they are more significant movements of growth. All the same, these daily steps are a transformational calling and they started with these well-intentioned cards.

Specifically, the very first card I picked up said,

Resolution: (Side One)

"We can be inspired by the fact that great things happen when men wake up and step up. When a man finally understands his role and resolutely surrenders himself to God's plan, his life completely changes. His priorities and vision become clear, and his life takes on a bold, new purpose."

2 Samuel 10:12: (Flip Side)

"Be strong and let us show ourselves courageous for the sake of our people and for the cities of our God; and may the Lord do what is good in His sight."

I understood this message. But I realized that the intentional behavior modification being suggested as a result of the pithy verse from the Bible was not exactly the story described in 2 Samuel 10. I looked deeper into the entire chapter. I would often find the behavioral change not related to the complete context of the Scripture. I felt cheated. Am I not reading Holy Scripture of a history of a people called out by God himself, and now it is summarized on a plastic type card with "…a bold, new purpose"? One might shoehorn an agenda into that one verse, but the entire context wouldn't support this well-worded recommendation.

Here's a better example bringing me discontent.

Resolution: (Side One)

"Every man needs to identify and release any leftover childishness from his past. Childhood has come and gone. It's time to repent

of wanting to remain there, learn to act our age, and move on to the greater, better, and nobler things of men."

1 Corinthians 13:11: (Flip Side)

"When I was a child, I spoke as a child, I understood as a child, I thought as a child; but when I became a man, I put away childish things."

This was about day 30 of systematically processing through the cards. While the message is not "bad," it wasn't fitting to the Scriptures. Do the ends justify the means in Christian culture? This one was most upsetting. After seeing this pattern and being disappointed, I switched to reading the "context," which in this case was 1 Corinthians 13.

It turns out, the entire chapter is about LOVE, not about being a child or a man.

Discontent With Simple Answers

This discontent drove me to go deeper. I thought if I'm going to have to "fight" with these cards, I might as well read the entire chapter. I determined I would find a more meaningful way to engage with the Scriptures, one that I could reason with in my mind. I did not feel comfortable getting a very loosely supported instruction.

And that sparked my decision to read these New Testament books in a different way: not a verse here or a verse there, but simply read them all. I wondered, is there a message that I'm missing by picking out isolated verses, analogous to examining the bark on the trees and not seeing the forest? And it wasn't that I had never studied the Bible before. No, I had for 30 to 40 years now. In hindsight, I would say I never took a holistic approach.

The change was initiated by life circumstances, church changes, and these cards, which largely came from Paul's letters. It seemed odd to have so many ideas that were only loosely related. I decided I would learn more about this man, Paul. I researched what we knew about him and found that I might want to organize his writings in the order in which we believe he wrote them. My plan was to read one chapter, not just a verse, but a complete chapter every day. I made the choice to use a laptop and with the electronic versions of the Bible, I would copy and paste the chapters into an electronic document. I would then journal my thoughts and read the chapter I'd selected, highlighting not just a few words in a few verses, but the entire chapter.

I started this process at the end of 2013 and continue to follow it today. I needed this routine to seek the big picture, message of what took place.

For now, my questions were: What is being addressed? What is being communicated? What were the circumstances or events that were driving Paul to write what he was writing? And even more basic, who was this guy? Where did he come from and who did he hang out with? For those who might be wondering, I approach the Scriptures in the traditional way, as the inerrant Word of God, inspired by God. But I want to put some structure around my reading.

The Top 100

I counted all the chapters of Paul's writing, 100 chapters (complete list shown in Table 1). That would be about three months of reading. I also noticed that he mostly wrote to churches that he visited on his missionary journeys. And these missionary journeys, along with Paul's conversion from Saul, were recorded in the book of Acts.

Table 1

Approximate Year	Letter/Book	Chapters
53-55	Galatians	6
53	1 Thessalonians	5
53	2 Thessalonians	3
57	1 Corinthians	16
57	2 Corinthians	13
58	Romans	16
62	Ephesians	6
62	Philippians	4
62	Colossians	4
63	Philemon	1
65	Hebrews	13
65	Titus	3
65	1 Timothy	6
67	2 Timothy	4
		100

The book of Acts, written by Luke, records the early history of this growing faith, which resulted from the difficult-to-observe Crucifixion, the amazing Resurrection, and surprising Ascension. The 28 chapters of Acts added a month to the reading plan, now a total of 128 chapters. I ventured in and treated it as a daily mission to which quickly became a habit. I did it mostly in the mornings, but I would adjust to evenings when my schedule required. I had my laptop nearby and opened up my journal document to record the date and time. I would write a bit about what was going on in my mind, events that were happening in my life. It wasn't simply about learning facts but considering the context: Who are these people, what's taking place? I wasn't attempting to create a systematic theology. I was simply asking "what do these words say?" and wanting to understand how they are connected to each other. Who was doing what to whom? And why were these stories and events presented as they were? I entered in with a questioning mind, which made each reading fresh.

The Study Bible Confusion

I striped out all types of annotations and cross references that one typically finds in a study Bible. I wanted to simply read, as if sent to my community. I suppose what I started is not what is traditionally known as "Bible study." It was simpler. I didn't have a guidebook; I didn't have small numbers and letters next to words directing me to other texts. I had simple biblical text, as it was translated, and I chose the New American Standard Bible.

I soon appreciated starting with the Book of Acts. Let me share my observations. The Ascension, Acts 1. Jesus departs. He has been resurrected and if we pay attention to what is going on, we can see that it takes place 40 days after the Resurrection. He told the disciples that had been with him, among whom was Peter. Peter denied Jesus while he was on trial. Jesus told them to wait for the Holy Spirit, for Power to come on them. He instructed them to return the short journey to Jerusalem and wait.

They thought Jesus would return soon, perhaps even the next day or week, but He reminded them that it wasn't for them to know exactly when. Even after seeing him resurrected, the disciples were still observing and not fully understanding what was taking place. It's been a long time, right? Nearly 2,000 years now.

Pentecost—The Overlooked Event

Then magic, Acts 2. It all changes. Jews from afar were in town for the 50 days after the Passover celebration. The Jewish celebration is called Shavuot, but the name it had at the time was Pentecost. Yet how often had I read Acts 2 and simply thought, "When the day of Pentecost came…." It wasn't simply discussing that particular day. It was the Jewish celebration of the giving of the 10 Commandments. Moses had been on Mount Sinai and brought the Word of God to the people 50 days after the first Passover.

Just prior to Jesus departing, He gave these instructions concerning the coming Holy Spirit in John 14:12–15:

> [12] Truly, truly, I say to you, he who believes in Me, the works that I do, he will do also; and greater *works* than these he will do; because I go to the Father. [13] Whatever you ask in My

name, that will I do, so that the Father may be glorified in the Son. ¹⁴ If you ask Me anything in My name, I will do *it*.

¹⁵ "If you love Me, you will keep My commandments.

Under what power would these "greater works" be accomplished?

John 14:16–17, 25–31

¹⁶ I will ask the Father, and He will give you another <u>Helper</u>, that He may be with you forever; ¹⁷ *that is* <u>the Spirit of truth</u>, whom the world cannot receive, because it does not see Him or know Him, *but* you know Him because <u>He abides with you</u> and <u>will be in you</u>.

²⁵ "These things I have spoken to you while abiding with you. ²⁶ But <u>the Helper, the Holy Spirit,</u> whom the Father <u>will send</u> in My name, <u>He will teach you</u> all things, and bring to your remembrance all that I said to you. ²⁷ Peace I leave with you; My peace I give to you; not as the world gives do I give to you. Do not let your heart be troubled, nor let it be fearful. ²⁸ You heard that I said to you, 'I go away, and I will come to you.' If you loved Me, you would have rejoiced because I go to the Father, for the Father is greater than I. ²⁹ Now I have told you before it happens, so that when it happens, you may believe. ³⁰ I will not speak much more with you, for the ruler of the world is coming, and he has nothing in Me; ³¹ but so that the world may know that I love the Father, I do exactly as the Father commanded Me. Get up, let us go from here.

John 16:5–15

⁵ "But now I am going to Him who sent Me; and none of you asks Me, 'Where are You going?' ⁶ But because I have said these things to you, sorrow has filled your heart. ⁷ But I tell you the truth, *it is to your advantage that I go away*; for if I do not go away, *the Helper* will not come to you; but if I go, I will send Him to you. ⁸ And He, when He comes, will convict the world concerning sin and righteousness and judgment; ⁹ concerning sin, because they do not believe in Me; ¹⁰ and concerning righteousness, because I go to the Father and you no longer see Me; ¹¹ and concerning judgment, because the ruler of this world has been judged.

¹² "I have many more things to say to you, but you cannot bear *them* now. ¹³ But when *He*, *the Spirit of truth*, comes, *He* will guide you into all the truth; for *He* will not speak on His own initiative, but whatever *He* hears, *He* will speak; and *He* will disclose to you what is to come. ¹⁴ *He* will glorify Me, for *He* will take of Mine and will disclose *it* to you. ¹⁵ All things that the Father has are Mine; therefore I said that *He* takes of Mine and will disclose *it* to you.

This Holy Spirit, He explained to His disciples was going to empower them to fully understand and do amazing things. Things even greater than Jesus himself.

It caught them by surprise. Yet, we see Peter who had denied Jesus three times, and even though restored by Jesus after the Resurrection, he wasn't fully empowered to make his proclamation in Acts 2 until the Holy Spirit came upon him. Some falsely claim that it was simply Peter seeing the resurrected Jesus that empowered him. But that experience of Peter's occurred 50 days prior and he was not proclaiming the gospel until the Holy Spirit filled him with the boldness to preach the first message. That may be a small point, but I say it reveals the difficulty many have in acknowledging the work of the Holy Spirit.

As Luke records the events, we see the leaders of this movement experiencing the Holy Spirit. God was working through Peter and John. I began to see that it was the Holy Spirit that was acting. As Peter, John, and others are in prison, "suddenly" God intervenes. Is it possible that this "suddenly" is a reminder that God is alive today and He is able and will intervene at any moment?

Acts: Unleashing Of The Holy Spirit

We arrive at Acts 6, 7, and 8 and Stephen's experience is described. He was selected to assist with the growth of this new way with God. Stephen was commissioned because some of the Hellenistic Jews complained that their widows were not being supported. These details are only necessary to explain how Stephen came to be in a position within this movement. Luke records what took place in logical format. Stephen would be called on to explain his views before an angry mob. Saul would stand by and approve Stephen's stoning.

Soon after, Saul was on his way to bring back followers of Jesus residing in Damascus. Yet, in Acts 9, God again chose to intervene. Saul was called out by Jesus and begins his journey of transformation from Pharisee/Jew, to baptized, Spirit-filled, Paul.

Later, we will observe several missionary journeys. Paul visited cities in today's Turkey, regions of Galatia, and then

Philippi, Thessalonica, Berea, Athens, Corinth, Ephesus, and back to Jerusalem.

We follow along step-by-step and ask, what's happening? What's God doing with Paul, Silas, Mark, Apollos, Lydia, Priscila, Aquila, Philip, and the many other men and women with whom God was working by His Holy Spirit? Luke is recording events that were taking place around these men and women called into living a new life with God.

Acts ends, with Paul in Rome in prison. It's the overview of the beginnings and Paul's life.

The Sixth Sola Method

Now I researched the timing of events and letters/books. We have these New Testament writings, but how were they placed in their order, and should we care? Are there scholars who tell us when they were written? And if so, what if we chose to read them in that order and reference back to Acts to follow the events and cities to which Paul traveled, considering the time and space between events?

The first letters were to the Galatians, 1 and 2 Thessalonians, 1 and 2 Corinthians, and then the Romans. And by organizing them in this manner and reviewing Paul's path, I recognized that the book of Romans ends with Paul's commitment that he would be going to Rome—only he had no idea that it would be after two to three years of imprisonment in Israel, followed by travel under guard on a ship that would be destroyed in a storm near the island of Malta.

We are invited to enter into God's plan, as God is working in and through His people. For example, when Paul wrote to Thessalonica, the words are not simply "quotable" instructions from God that are to be transported to the present, but a record of what God was doing at that time. They are the observations and instructions from Paul to the people he was addressing about a relationship with God. These events show us how the living God worked in the past, which brought me to ask, "Is God active as He was in those days?"

Holy Spirit The New Jesus?

My experiences and thoughts about God's presence in my moment-by-moment living were incorporated and questioned in light how God worked in these initial years. I would ask myself about how a particular chapter might have something to say about today's circumstances. I cycled through these 128 chapters in about four months and decided to repeat.

What I observed was how often the Holy Spirit was the actor and was working through people. These words were no longer individual passages but a whole recording of what was happening at that time.

I would consider this rich context and see if there was a message for me today. Peter, John, Philip, Barnabas, Paul were all moved by the Holy Spirit. My discontent was why do we skip over the subject of the Holy Spirit and so often assume we know what the right thing to do is from our intellect, our knowledge? Is not the message that we have a Living God that has provided and sent His Holy Spirit to us? Do we treat the Word of God more like a "law book" even though much of it is attempting to get away from the Jewish "Law"?

While all this was playing out, my local church was going through a transition. I have attended a church service nearly every Sunday, and my 40-year habit was to expect a word of instruction, encouragement, or exhortation. In hindsight, I expected too much from these messages. Most pastors are excellent speakers and they often present teachings and convincing messages that we should consider. However, I, and possibly we, have put too high an expectation on these once-a-week gatherings.

I had been at a church for about 15 years. The original pastor was retiring, and a search committee was determining the next candidate. Perhaps a change would be a benefit to us all.

The Vision Caster

The selected pastor was a mid-30s, enthusiastic Southern Baptist from the "Bible Belt." The church itself, I later realized, was a part of this denomination. I'm not one for church denominations, but I would later learn that my bluntness was not received well.

I don't recall the comments I was making, but one was about a new mission statement. I thought the statement was a bit "works" oriented, as if we could carry out the mission without God and the Holy Spirit's involvement. From my independent reading, I wanted to have more Holy Spirit, but here was a "Mission Statement" ironically not even referencing the Holy Spirit of God. There was not much interest in my line of questioning and that's when my frustration arose. I am still learning. I understand I can do better at approaching subjects that are of interest to me but may not be of interest to others.

Because I had established my own habit of reading every day, I came to realize that there was something missing in the messages

I was hearing and not just at my church. I thought I should pay attention to other churches. Today, the internet allows anyone to get a live look in on what is happening worldwide. I was seeing a pattern of emphasis on being right, of having the right beliefs, and just generally a clinical view of our faith.

As I read, I began to recognize the phrase, "power of the Holy Spirit," which frequently occurred in the chapters I was reading. Yet in the commentary there were only brief mentions of the Holy Spirit, as if we should all know. My increasing attention to references to the Holy Spirit was brought forth through the confluence of my daily experience and the frequency of these words. On the one hand, it was good that I recognized I was placing too much importance on the Sunday morning messages. There is often encouragement to "spend time in the Word," but what does that really mean? It's a big book. Should we just open it up randomly and start reading, and where to go next? How are all these writings related to each other? Is there a core message running through it? And how would we find it?

I wasn't hearing anything resembling what Paul described as walking in the Spirit. I don't believe we had a series in many years from "Galatians." And by series, that's the cultural norm with which I was familiar. We'd spend several weeks on Hebrews, or some other book and topic at the discretion of the leadership.

And that's when I began to see that I needed to hear from all of the Scriptures and not be dependent solely on Sunday morning teachings. Perhaps this is obvious to the reader, but I look back on it now and see that my expectations had been extremely high for the leadership of this church.

Putting My Puzzle Together

I was "confirmed" in the Lutheran church, which my father never attended. He would, however, attend faithfully to his Roman Catholic services, setting up a bit of confusion on the organized religion front. It is likely why I am feeling so compelled to comment on the state of reformation and faith.

Sunday morning teachers could do more to demonstrate how we can all participate in the truths of the entire message of the Bible by committing to reading daily. They may believe they are doing so, yet my observation is it's more about teaching and leading into exhortation, even if there is little or no exhortation in the text.

On a personal front, I am more "exhorting" myself or allowing the Scriptures to exhort me each day. I'm reading this daily in a fashion that builds the narrative. Quite often, the "spending time in the Word" revolved around a program, such as "read the Bible in a year," but those are monumental tasks, and I preferred to focus on the now, even if it was 2,000 years old and not 3,000. What I stumbled onto was focusing on the risen Christ and what the Holy Spirit began to do 2,000 years ago and to think about how that may be continuing today.

Yes, reading Genesis is certainly beneficial, but since we are in the period of having the Holy Spirit present with us, it is important that we incorporate that Holy Spirit power, and understand its impact on our daily living in hope, faith, and love.

A Spiritual Coach?

When I started a fitness training program, focusing on lifting, the personal trainer would guide me through six to eight exercises in about 50 to 60 minutes, and that was a good day's workout. I would return two other days and repeat what I learned. Until I had that personal trainer explain what to do, how to do it, and the right effort and commitment, I would have entered with confusion and no plan to "get this exercise thing" figured out. And that experience brought me to a realization that just instructing, teaching, exhorting is insufficient to build spiritual resilience, perseverance, muscle, if you will. Perhaps we need more coaching from Christian leadership.

Why do we utilize little, if any personal training or coaching in our spiritual practices or disciplines? Sure, there are great books and devotionals, but what about modeling what we say we believe? Is that not where we best honor and walk in a manner worthy of the Lord? Some may call discipleship a form of coaching, but the programs are often prepared meals as opposed to learning how to cook and prepare our own. Many discipleship programs are more of the same, reading a book at a time, and not as much about viewing the message and walking in the Spirit. It may be that we believe we are doing that, but we often get distracted by details that differentiate one reformed denomination or belief from another.

I compare my chronological reading of Scripture, following what the Holy Spirit had done in the early church and especially Paul's life, to a gym workout. With this view Paul became something like my personal trainer. It's a form of discipline to read, get the message, and return back again. I read Galatians, two to three experiences a year. That's similar to getting a balance of bench pressing and other pushing exercises with other days of pulling. Days with Acts, Hebrews, and Romans brought balance to the entire message.

My reading of Galatians prompted me to consider where the fruit of the Spirit should, could, and later was showing up in my life. How is the fruit of the Spirit appearing in my relationships with others and even my relationship with myself? Paul explains the choice to walk in the flesh or walk in the Spirit. This repeating and returning to Galatians revealed how much I needed and wanted the fruit of the Spirit to manifest in my relationships.

Work It Daily

My Six Sola Method is the start of my day. It's about 30 minutes, recording thoughts and moving through the text. If I was in Galatians 1 on Monday, and read each day, I would be at Galatians 5 on Friday. That's a week of thinking about works, faith, and grace in the context of the book of Galatians. The recurring themes of the chapters helped me to live out the calling in different situations.

With that said, my relationships with others did not always evidence love, joy, peace, patience, kindness, goodness, faithfulness, and self-control. I notice that when I'm not living and walking in the Spirit, I exhibit less of these attitudes and behaviors. I humbly realized that I am not demonstrating high levels of the fruit of the Spirit. Later in the book, I integrated a mathematical concept that we are all familiar with, that takes the pressure off to be "good enough" and just focus on improvement, not meeting others' expectations.

I recognize my need for personal transformation. I respect the Scriptures, I understand the doctrine of faith alone, but something was missing—this walking in the Spirit. I was thinking more about the Reformation, the coming 500th anniversary, and that's how I came upon my need, and my suggestion: All of us need transformation. We can argue about doctrines, beliefs, the Scriptures, but what good is it?

I needed to grow in what the Scriptures call sanctification and I believe it is only through walking in the Holy Spirit that I will transform. Thus, the concept of Sola Spiritu Ambulatio formed.

Ready For Some Latin? Spiritu Ambulatio

My call to action is to walk in the Spirit as Paul describes. I hesitate here as it may appear to you that I ignore other Scriptures, and I want to assure you this is not an idea that is isolated only by reviewing Paul's writings. I believe he forms a core framework, yet for example, we see in John's gospel that Jesus told the disciples that the Holy Spirit was coming. As I mentioned earlier in John chapters 14–17, His last 24 hours before the Crucifixion, He introduces to His disciples what could only be a mystery, and that is when Jesus spoke of this coming Helper/Holy Spirit. Now those 12 disciples heard it, John later records it, and yet further writings confirm that even though Jesus made statements, the disciples often did not understand.

I occasionally ask myself, "Do you realize what you are suggesting? You are suggesting walking in the Spirit. Do you know how general and vague this is?" And yes, I do see how challenging this is to discuss.

If you are hearing numerous calls to serve at your church, mission, religious organization, nonprofit, and yet don't feel like you are gifted in those activities and feel a bit alone in your own church, keep reading. I suggest the Sola Spiritu Ambulatio is a way to deepen the Great Relationship with God and the Holy Spirit. I am taking the role of coach or guide, knowing full well that the Spirit is the real guide.

This has been my discontent with the systems I fell into, and how I was working my way out to a better way. After a few times through, I read and recognized the numerous references to the Holy Spirit. That was the initiation of the Spiritu Ambulatio.

CHAPTER 3

THE GREAT RELATIONSHIP

My spiritual workouts consist of reading a chapter a day, moving from the chronological order of events, with the book of Acts being an overview and connection point for many of Paul's letters. I journal and pray about my circumstances. I observe what God has done in the past days and how He may be directing me today. My desire is to consider what God is calling me to do instead of telling others what they need to do. Believe me, that is a significant transformation.

Looking back on six years of daily practice, the personal transformations may be small, but I believe there's progress, one step at a time. There are many devotionals, men and women who have expressed their thoughts and experiences on the pages of many excellent books. For me, my mind has a difficult time considering how to bring an experience of someone I don't know well, and perhaps even from a different culture, which drives me to simply read what we have before us in the Scriptures.

One of the results of following the plan I'm describing is that you begin to build your own "live devotional." It is unique to your life, your gifts, and your calling. You have your own heroic challenges you face, sometimes many over the course of a single day. How better to overcome those challenges than to remember that God's presence is with you. Often the drive for meaning and purpose is summarized as finding that "one thing." This may put stress on our minds as we consider what that "one thing" might be.

His Presence

And yet, God promised the Holy Spirit would be with us and that through the Spirit, we are in His presence always. Writing your own journal is a devotional way to connect with this presence of the Holy Spirit. Write down what you observe. What are your thoughts? Too often, we pick up a study guide and have others influence our thoughts. This is a time to get rid of those distractions. God has gifted us with an amazing mind to figure out what is next.

For me, I added a few books from the New Testament that were not written by Paul. The most significant reading that has adjusted my view on the Scriptures is John. After reading John's Epistles, and then understanding John's position as the "beloved disciple," it appears he had a more intimate relationship with Jesus. I suspect that we quite often view the 12 disciples as a homogenous group that Jesus picked out strategically because they all met some type of unifying minimum standards. I now believe He chose whom He chose because He could, and some had a more intimate relationship than others.

When it comes to Paul, he was not one of the twelve, and yet, he writes most of the New Testament. Because he was not one of the twelve, when I read what he did, and what he wrote, consider that he is more like you and me. We were not with Jesus like Peter, John, Matthew, Mark, and others. And even so, John stood out as this beloved disciple.

Forming The Foundation

Starting with Acts and reading Paul's writings, adding James's, Jude's, Peter's, and John's writings is another 21 days of reading. And after 128 days, why not another 21? The result was the complete core teaching, the working of the Holy Spirit in the rollout of the church. Now, the only books I don't include in my daily routine are Matthew, Mark, Luke, and most of John, and the book of Revelation. Please note, I find them all important and the Old Testament as well, but I want to walk in the Holy Spirit, to bring fruit to those in my presence and work toward those goals. That's why it's important to stick to this focused plan. Yes, reading a Psalm or a Proverb is important, but I frequently consider that we now have the indwelling power of God himself.

And it was in this expanded reading that I took an interest in John. Specifically, in 1 John 1:3 "…so that you too may have fellowship with us…", where John invites us into fellowship with him. It had to be a spiritual fellowship and that intrigued me enough to consider the gospel of John.

What is the current situation? We are not in the pre-Crucifixion era. We know the gospel. This book is not an evangelist message intending to present the facets of the faith; it is for those who have stepped into the faith, desiring to serve, yet who may not be in a position to confidently proceed with their calling. We may get so many messages that we end up in despair of not meeting the Vision cast by others, or the numerous virtue signals. If we could step back a moment and realize, the message can't be like this, can it? But we are not given the time with everyone else's agenda.

We have many distractions with our electronic connectivity. Everywhere we turn today, there is marketing. In religious circles, marketing is also quite present. There are messages to "sacrifice" ourselves through performing various services. These messages sometimes implore us to finish the Great Commission to "go" and do "evangelism." They may be directionally correct, but are they consistent with the actual message? Now they are not necessarily bad, but the push certainly leaves the impression that this life is all about doing and not being.

And on the gospels, I suggest a slightly different framework when reading them, and by that, I mean taking a bit deeper historical context than what we may traditionally have thought. When Jesus is teaching in the gospels, it's prior to the most amazing event, Crucifixion, Resurrection, Ascension, and coming Holy Spirit. No one could imagine what was about to happen, not even His closest disciples. He was going to experience amazing pain. There would be confusion, doubt of even a Resurrection, then His departure, and what about the Kingdom? Then this powerful wind. How could he teach that, other than to allude to it and let it be understood after the events?

To Whom Did Jesus Speak?

Jesus was speaking to mostly Jews, with their religion's history, and He was not "sending messages" to the future generations of "believers." This is not to say we ignore these words. Instead, I'm saying put them in the context of the environment in which they were spoken. It's why I focus on the post-Resurrection Scriptures—the Holy Spirit is here. We are walking in the presence of the living God, not the same old Sermon on the Mount. It's all new now. Perhaps that will upset some. I am still in agreement that it's all valid; I just ask is it really for Gentiles?

For example, shall we consider the rich young ruler. Today, this teaching is often brought out to encourage larger donations to the church. The moral of the story, at that time, is exactly as Jesus described it. Hanging onto riches makes it difficult to follow God or enjoy a life with God. Notice at this time, Jesus is not speaking of how the man forfeited abundant life. It was more of a commentary on, what I would say, were the Jewish norms of the day. To obtain eternal life for this Jew, Jesus is instructing him to give it all away. It made sense at that moment, for that person. But is that not more of a particular situation and not a universal truth?

What might have happened in the future with this rich young ruler as the next few years advanced? Is it not possible that after the events of the Crucifixion, Resurrection, Ascension, and coming Holy Spirit, that this man could have become a believer in Jesus? I say it is completely possible, and even likely, considering his amazing story. His encounter with Jesus may have changed everything for him.

Should this be a controversial view? The only result is that I suggest we read the Gospels bearing in mind that the Cross, the Resurrection, Ascension, and coming of the Holy Spirit has not taken place and listeners would not understand.

The Great Relationship

John wrote his Epistles in a very personal and informal manner. In John 21, John records how Jesus spoke with Peter and his famous restoration. Jesus asks Peter three times if Peter loved him. This is contrasted with the three times that Peter denied Him before the Crucifixion. The sermons on this subject usually end there, and the implied message is no matter how many times we may have denied Jesus, He is able to forgive us. And that's not a poor message. However, there's more to the story as John continues.

Immediately after the restoration, we have Jesus explaining to Peter what will happen to him in the future. Peter is recorded as commenting, "What's going to happen to John?" And this is rather shocking. Here, we have Peter in what we believe is his restored relationship with Jesus, and immediately it appears that he is falling back in some way. This is clear by how Jesus responded to Peter's question about John.

Jesus says, "What is that to you? You follow me!"

This is a rather sharp rebuke. And is this a significant event? Well, keep reading and we see the conclusion of John's Gospel. How does the disciple whom Jesus most loved end his Gospel? And remember, Matthew, Mark, and Luke have all been written. It's estimated that John wrote his gospel 20 to 25 years after the others.

John records that Jesus had done and said many things, and if he or others were to attempt to record them all, there wouldn't be enough books to do so. And that's it. We have restoration, rebuke, and infinite number of stories that could be told. Let's ask the question, why does John end with this interaction with Peter?

In many respects, this would be considered the last words of Jesus to His disciples. Is it fair to consider that he may have a more personal, a more emotional connection with Jesus?

Here, John carefully records this encounter between Peter and Jesus. John was present and overheard this discussion. I describe this as a call to the "Great Relationship." It is Jesus expressing to us, through the observation by John, that we are not to compare or set up boundary markers about what it looks like to be a follower of Jesus. John's recording of these events shows us Jesus calling us to simply follow him. Could there be any more important words with which to end the gospels?

Great Commission Before Great Relationship?

I contrast this with the common expression of the Great Commission, which is recorded by Matthew in his Gospel, yet here, John, the beloved disciple ends with a relationship event. Jesus is telling Peter to not compare himself to John, that Peter needs to follow Jesus and not to get involved in what John or anyone else may be called to do. Throughout this book, my opinion is that the Great Commission will take care of itself if we all join in the Great Relationship with God himself through His Holy Spirit. From this foundation, all service and ministry flows from our core being with our own unique core skills and strengths that God himself created in us, not someone else. Thus, there's no fear that God is not alive and that His Holy Spirit is not effectual.

Recall, I didn't start with John. I was interested in Paul. But because of my reading and cycling back for another run-through, I was driven to John 21. My challenge is how to describe walking in the Spirit.

The calls to action by preachers and teachers set out objectives for us. Yet here, Jesus simply says to follow him. Jesus calls Peter to a Great Relationship. Now it's going to be difficult, right? Jesus is ascending soon, and John, Peter, the others have no idea. Once the Ascension is completed, the only choice is to be walking in the Spirit. Jesus is no longer physically available to follow.

And that's where the Sixth Sola comes in. It's about walking in and walking with the Holy Spirit, which Jesus promised us. We will see in Acts and the other letters how this Holy Spirit begins to be present with Peter, John, and others. It's true, I'm suggesting we all need to walk in the Spirit. But how do we do that? Is it something to do? Or is it a presence of mind? Is it a conscious peace? Thoughts? What is it?

Walking in the Spirit (Sola Spiritu Ambulatio) is as important as Sola Scriptura and Sola Fide. These last words of Jesus to Peter, "What is that to you? You follow me!" have remained with me as an inspiring foundation for the Great Relationship.

My self-awareness and the pull to get "it" right has me reflecting on the need to move on from the reformation of others to my own transformation. This is what will impact those around me. I'm convinced this comes from the moment-by-moment acknowledgement of God's presence.

The naming of the "Great Relationship" didn't just happen. It was the result of journaling through the events of the New Testament. The observing of the "What is that to you? You follow me!" was not from looking for it. It came to me from the desire to integrate what I am experiencing in my life with the amazing mystery we have been given to share this life with God and others.

You Are The Hero

We all have challenges. When writing, I referenced the story framework consisting of a hero, a challenge, a guide, a plan, and a call to action. This framework is efficient for organizing fiction or even our own lives, and yet here, it is also a great way to describe this Spiritu Ambulatio.

You are the hero. You are invested in responding to multiple challenges. If you picked up this book, it is possible that a challenge or several are driving you to find or execute your calling. I'm here to guide, but I'm not the Guide. I am pointing to the Spirit as this ultimate Guide for us.

The call to action is to give up reforming others and begin a practice of transformation.

My original reading practice started with the book of Acts. But then I realized John 21 was too good, so why not throw in John 20. This is what I do every day, cycle through one chapter a day, and it gives a broader context for understanding what was happening. I believe you will begin to see a benefit to reading in this way. And with that, let me share how I came upon my views by starting with an overview of the book of Acts.

CHAPTER 4

IN THE BEGINNING WAS THE HOLY SPIRIT: THE BOOK OF ACTS CHAPTERS 1-5

I gave the briefest of overviews of Acts, now let us slow it down a bit. We normally think of Genesis, and John when we read, "In the Beginning was the Word." Here I'm reminding us that we believe in the Trinity, and that means the Holy Spirit is actually the one and same as God and Jesus.

My initial plan was to read the book of Acts, as this is the beginning of the unleashing of the Holy Spirit. Luke wrote his gospel. He then told us what happened in the days, weeks, and months after the Ascension. Luke will join Paul much later in Paul's missionary journeys. Acts is a chronological history and I would estimate Luke joined Paul in Acts chapter 16 or later. Therefore, Luke was busy digging into the history of not only Jesus for his gospel account, but also all the details we have recorded from the book of Acts.

We estimate Luke joined Paul when his language changes from "they" to "we." The actual dates, cities are not important at the moment. I only wanted to point out that Luke was certainly influenced by Paul. Also, for Luke's gospel, since Paul was not one of the twelve disciples, he must have taken an occasion to get details from Peter, John, or James, for example. Luke is a researcher of these events and explains what was taking place.

Luke connects his gospel with this "second volume," at the time of the Ascension. From the beginning, Luke explains how Jesus calls His disciples to the Mount of Olivet and informs them that they will be His witnesses as He prepares to depart. He then instructs them to wait for the power that the Father promised. Notice the language: It's not an imperative, but a simple matter of fact. You will be my witnesses.

The Lost Spiritual Gift Of Evangelism

It raises the question if many of the programs that are designed and structured to encourage people to "give away their faith" or "share the gospel" differ from the spirit of what's described here—that we will be His witnesses, some with formal words and some with words of love, kindness, and gentleness. While some may say "evangelism" is for everyone, I prefer to believe everyone is a witness.

And the best witnesses are those filled with the Holy Spirit. The explanation of the gospel is facts and knowledge oriented, but empathetically listening and engaging with people is a demonstration of love, gentleness, kindness. Some have said, "People don't care what you know until they know how much you care." Many of us have heard the message to "go" and we "must preach" and that "faith comes from hearing." All good, but watch the virtue signaling. God is able to speak to each of us through His Holy Spirit in every moment of every day, and that's my goal in communicating with you. I think most of us can relate because some have said 95 percent of us don't "do evangelism" the way "they say." Whatever that means?

In Acts 1, they asked if Jesus was coming soon to restore His Kingdom, but that is not for them to know, nor for us. Reading between the lines, Jesus might be a bit frustrated with the last 40 days. He's been crucified, likely not a pleasant experience, buried, risen, and appeared to many people. It's almost like He might be thinking, "Guys, isn't this enough? I've told you what was going to happen. You didn't believe me. It all happened, and it's a miracle that I'm alive. You still don't get it, and I'm departing now, and wait as the Holy Spirit will come."

They return to Jerusalem, only about a mile from the Mount of Olivet.

Acts 2 begins with the words, "When the day of Pentecost had come..." indicating that this was a special day. I had mistaken this as a foreshadowing of coming events, but Pentecost is a historic Jewish celebration. It's Shavuot, which takes place 50 days after the Jewish Passover.

This is a celebration of God giving the 10 Commandments to Moses on Mount Sinai and is God's instructions to His people in written form. In this year, Jesus had ascended 10 days earlier, and we have the coming of the Holy Spirit. This connects the symbolism of Passover/Jesus to tablets/Spirit.

People observing this "new" Pentecost see what are described as "tongues of fire" from above, coming down onto the disciples assembled in the streets of Jerusalem. It is recorded that Jews coming from all over the region in the city for this Jewish celebration were hearing messages from God through this Holy Spirit.

Peter Filled

This is the Holy Spirit moving amongst people. That's the message from this fourth day of reading. Peter was filled with the Spirit and he spoke boldly. Others were moved by the same Holy Spirit to join with the original disciples in this new faith as the Holy Spirit allowed more and more people to understand what Jesus's recent Crucifixion, Resurrection, and Ascension meant for them. The Holy Spirit is the one that is now writing the Scriptures on their hearts. This was foretold in the Old Testament, hundreds of years earlier, only now it was happening amongst them.

And Peter changes. He's over his comparison to John and filled with this mysterious Holy Spirit. He proclaims what he experienced with Jesus and the understanding he now has with the present filling by the Holy Spirit. It was not simply an intellectual understanding that waited until this moment. Acts 2:14 was all about the Holy Spirit and not seeing the risen Jesus 50 days earlier. Mixing the two might be considered false teaching, but I digress.

In Acts 3, the Holy Spirit is again working through Peter and John.

> But Peter, along with John, fixed his gaze on him and said, "Look at us!" And he *began* to give them his attention, expecting to receive something from them. But Peter said, "I do not possess silver and gold, but <u>what I do have</u> I give to you: In the name of Jesus Christ the Nazarene—walk!"

The man is healed. The religious leaders are not pleased and in Acts 4 the story continues.

> **4** As they were speaking to the people, the priests and the captain of the temple *guard* and the Sadducees came up to them, ² being greatly disturbed because they were teaching the people and <u>proclaiming in Jesus the Resurrection from the dead</u>. ³ And they laid hands on them and put them in jail until the next day, for it was already evening.

> They were greatly disturbed and had them arrested. They were brought out for questioning the next day and, ⁸ Then Peter, <u>*filled with the Holy Spirit*</u>,

> Peter spoke with boldness once more and,

> ¹³ Now as they observed the confidence of Peter and John and understood that they were uneducated and untrained men, they were amazed, and *began* to recognize them as <u>having been with Jesus</u>.

Peter and John were bold and confident, and yet they were uneducated and untrained. How often do we believe we are not good enough to speak up or believe we don't have enough knowledge? It is the Holy Spirit facilitating these events. It's not Peter and John's planning.

This is an example of walking in the Spirit. Luke doesn't name this explicitly, yet are there any other words to describe what's happening? We may take courage and guidance from knowing that the Spirit will give us the words. Later, we will see that we are called to love people. That's a commandment from Jesus himself: Love God and love others. When we lead with love, the opportunity to be moved to speak is going to increase.

The pressure remained on Peter, and John and the others, who had not been arrested, were concerned.

> ³¹ And when they had prayed, the place where they had gathered together was shaken, and they were <u>*all filled with the Holy Spirit*</u> and *began* to speak the Word of God with boldness.

The Holy Spirit is demonstrating His capability to fill us with boldness to speak of the mystery of the gospel. You may be hearing others pressure you into doing what amounts to cold calling these days, but our rightfully respected Peter and John are not speaking from a place of intellectual knowledge. They simply are living and speaking to the events that they have witnessed the last few weeks. It's fresh. Can we be as authentic as Peter and John? Could we be getting in our own way, thinking the gospel is complicated and we need to have answers for all sorts of issues?

God With Us Life

If we encourage one another to walk in the Spirit at every moment, we will display more love, joy, peace, patience, gentleness, kindness, goodness, faithfulness, and self-control. We need more of us living strong in our faith that God and especially

His Holy Spirit is with us. Would it be better if we encouraged one another to be filled with the Spirit instead of emphasizing knowledge-based evangelism?

In Acts 5, we see image management. A husband and wife apparently wanted to be more pious than they were, and they were struck down—a warning for all of us tempted to make an impression on others.

Next, the apostles are arrested once again.

[17] But the high priest rose up, along with all his associates (that is the sect of the Sadducees), and they were filled with jealousy. [18] They laid hands on the apostles and put them in a public jail.

And next,

[19] But during the night an angel of the Lord opened the gates of the prison, and taking them out he said, [20] "Go, stand and speak to the people in the temple the whole message of this Life."

Here, God is active, fully capable of intervening and this time through the spiritual being of an angel. There's spiritual activity happening with these leaders as the message of the Crucifixion, Resurrection, Ascension, and coming of the Holy Spirit goes out amongst the people. It is worth pausing here to ask what "this Life" might mean to Luke, Peter, and John.

The faith is impacting more and more people of Jerusalem. It would soon move beyond the city limits. The Holy Spirit is the one making all these events possible. Is not this same Holy Spirit active today?

The next large excerpt of Scripture continues describing how the Holy Spirit is "unleashed," which may not be the best description, as it appears God and His Holy Spirit is being strategic in how this new faith is to spread. It starts with the Jews, the disciples, and in Jerusalem.

Forest From The Trees

This is the beginning of this promised Holy Spirit's work. We often will consider three to four verses in a chapter for 30 minutes. However, reading larger "chunks," for lack of a better word, and looking for threads that may be flowing through the text is part of the "forest" view of what the message is about. I thought it best to continue on with this method as way of example of how I read and what I observe. With that, let's move on and we will soon be introduced to Saul and his conversion to Paul.

CHAPTER 5

SAUL TO PAUL TO PHILIP TO PETER, ACTS 6–10

My motivations are to pay close attention to who Paul is as a person and what he has to say. Recall, Luke is writing this book. He later comes into a relationship with Paul and is essentially researching this history from Paul, Peter, and John.

I ask myself why Jesus does not choose to have Saul/Paul be one of His disciples. This is based on God being all knowing. If He plans for so much of the New Testament to be written by Paul, why not have his story begin as one of the twelve? He is the right age, within five to ten years of the others.

My theory is that the 12 disciples are called, not from the city of Jerusalem, but Galilee. These are fishermen and tax collectors who grew up in the rural areas 80 miles from Jerusalem. These men are not educated in the best schools of Israel. And yet we know Saul is studying with the top Jewish teachers of the law. It's possible that Jesus doesn't want to be debating with Saul as he travels.

Regardless, Saul is advancing in the Jewish religion. He is a Pharisee and is respected by the leaders in Jerusalem. As the church grows, Saul joins and leads efforts to arrest and constrain the Jews that are being influenced by this movement. The growing numbers with faith are chosen and come to understand what Jesus had done, did, and even what he continues to do. They believe Peter, John, others as they explain how Jesus fulfilled the prophecies from their Scriptures and prophets of their past. This is the Jewish faith expanding, and Saul is working to limit the impact on the Jewish faith that had dominated the region for centuries.

We are introduced to Saul through Stephen. In Acts 6, Stephen is added to the church organizational leadership as a servant, yet he speaks eloquently, and when challenged by the Jewish leadership he speaks boldly.

In Acts 7, Stephen is asked to speak to these Jewish leaders. He presents the history with which they are familiar, the Jewish history and how it connects with the events of the past few months.

> [51] "You men who are stiff-necked and uncircumcised in heart and ears are always <u>*resisting the Holy Spirit*</u>; you are doing just as your fathers did. [52] Which one of the prophets did your fathers not persecute? They killed those who had previously announced the coming of the Righteous One, whose <u>*betrayers and murderers you have now become*</u>; [53] you who received the law as ordained by angels, and *yet* did not keep it."

54 Now when they heard this, they were <u>cut to the quick</u>, and they *began* gnashing their teeth at him. **55** But being <u>*full of the Holy Spirit*</u>, he gazed intently into heaven and saw the glory of God, and Jesus standing at the right hand of God; **56** and he said, "Behold, I see the heavens opened up and the Son of Man standing at the right hand of God." **57** But they cried out with a loud voice, and covered their ears and rushed at him with one impulse. **58** When they had driven him out of the city, they *began* stoning *him*; and the witnesses laid aside their robes at the feet of <u>*a young man named Saul.*</u> **59** They went on stoning Stephen as he called on *the Lord* and said, "Lord Jesus, receive my spirit!" **60** Then falling on his knees, he cried out with a loud voice, "Lord, do not hold this sin against them!" Having said this, he fell asleep.

Stephen comments that they are resisting the Holy Spirit. They are circumcised in the flesh, but notice, not in the heart. This is the coming of the Holy Spirit. The Holy Spirit chooses to open people's eyes, minds, and hearts. Stephen recognizes that it was God that brought Jesus to earth, to die, resurrect, and ascend.

Yet, boldly Stephen declares that the men about to stone him are resisting this power, this truth, this bringer of understanding and faith. They don't get it. What don't we get?

The tipping point for these Jews, to the point of anger and eventual stoning, is not the comment about resisting the Holy Spirit, but being accused of the betrayal and murder of Jesus.

Do We Need More Knowledge?

Consider what might be going on in Saul's mind. We don't have direct statements that Saul was aware of the Crucifixion of Jesus, yet it does not seem that out of line to believe that Saul was very familiar with the end of Jesus's life, His Resurrection, and even the events, the months prior to Pentecost. Then he witnesses Stephen proclaim the news of Jesus and how it is all connected with the teachings of Judaism.

Saul must have had an intellectual understanding. And to see anyone preach and stand by their convictions in the face of strong opposition, one would think it must have left an impression on Saul. However, it is as if nothing out of the ordinary is taking place.

Acts 8 begins with the conclusive statement of Saul's view at that moment, he is "in hearty agreement with putting him to death." This leads to the widespread persecution of those associated with this new faith or way. Still, the apostles are not chased away, but stay in Jerusalem.

This continues in Acts 8:

> ⁴ Therefore, those who had been scattered went about preaching the word. ⁵ Philip went down to the city of Samaria and *began* proclaiming Christ to them. ⁶ The crowds with one accord were giving attention to what was said by Philip, as they heard and saw the signs which he was performing. ⁷ For *in the case of* many who had unclean spirits, they were coming out *of them* shouting with a loud voice; and many who had been paralyzed and lame were healed. ⁸ So there was much rejoicing in that city.

Philip is simply moved to spread the gospel. The words of Jesus are fulfilled from Acts 1, and Philip is a witness in Samaria. It's supernatural, the Holy Spirit and angels are active.

These Scriptures demonstrate the power and working of the Holy Spirit. I am moved to simply include them and highlight specifics.

> [9] Now there was a man named _Simon_, who formerly was _practicing magic_ in the city and astonishing the people of Samaria, _claiming to be someone great_; [10] and they all, from smallest to greatest, were giving attention to him, saying, "_This man is what is called the Great Power of God_." [11] And they were giving him attention because he had for a long time astonished them with his magic arts. [12] _But_ when they _believed_ Philip preaching _the good news_ about the kingdom of God and the name of Jesus Christ, _they were being baptized_, men and women alike. [13] _Even Simon himself believed_; and after being baptized, he continued on with Philip, and as he observed signs and great miracles taking place, _he was constantly amazed_.
>
> [14] Now when the apostles in Jerusalem heard that Samaria had received the Word of God, _they sent them Peter and John_, [15] who came down and prayed for them _that they might receive the Holy Spirit_. [16] For He had _not yet fallen upon any of them_; they had simply been _baptized in the name of the Lord Jesus_. [17] Then they _began_ laying their hands on them, and _they were receiving the Holy Spirit_. [18] Now when _Simon_ saw that _the Spirit_ was bestowed through the laying on of the apostles' hands, _he offered them money_, [19] saying, "_Give this authority_

> *to me as well, so that everyone on whom I lay my hands may receive the Holy Spirit.*" ²⁰ But Peter said to him, "May your silver perish with you, because *you thought you could obtain the gift of God with money!* ²¹ You have no part or portion in this matter, for *your heart is not right before God.* ²² Therefore repent of this wickedness of yours, and pray the Lord that, if possible, *the intention of your heart may be forgiven you.* ²³ For I see that you are in the gall of bitterness and in the bondage of iniquity." ²⁴ But *Simon* answered and said, "*Pray to the Lord for me yourselves, so that nothing of what you have said may come upon me.*"

Simon believed he wanted the power, and wanted to "pay for it." Peter rebukes him for thinking he could purchase this power. We don't know what happened to Simon, but it's clear that one can believe in repentance, be baptized, and have the Holy Spirit. But as for having the ability like Peter, to "lay hands" on others, well, it doesn't look like Simon will be having that.

Next, there's more action from the living God through His Holy Spirit, angels, or both.

> ²⁶ But *an angel of the Lord* spoke to Philip saying, "Get up and go south to the road that descends from Jerusalem to Gaza." (This is a desert *road*.) ²⁷ So he got up and went; and there was an Ethiopian eunuch, a court official of Candace, queen of the Ethiopians, who was in charge of all her treasure; and he had come to Jerusalem to worship, ²⁸ and he was returning and sitting in his chariot, and was reading the prophet Isaiah. ²⁹ Then *the Spirit* said to Philip, "Go up and join this chariot." ³⁰ Philip ran up and heard him reading Isaiah

the prophet, and said, "Do you understand what you are reading?" ³¹ And he said, "Well, how could I, unless someone guides me?" And he invited Philip to come up and sit with him.

³⁴ The eunuch answered Philip and said, "Please *tell me*, of whom does the prophet say this? Of himself or of someone else?" ³⁵ Then Philip <u>opened his mouth</u> and beginning from this Scripture he <u>preached Jesus to him</u>. ³⁶ As they went along the road they came to some water; and the eunuch said, "Look! Water! What prevents me from being baptized?" ³⁷ And Philip said, "<u>If you believe with all your heart, you may</u>." And he answered and said, "I believe that Jesus Christ is the Son of God." ³⁸ And he ordered the chariot to stop; and they both went down into the water, Philip as well as the eunuch, and he baptized him. ³⁹ When they came up out of the water, <u>the Spirit of the Lord</u> snatched Philip away; and the eunuch no longer saw him, but went on his way rejoicing.

Acts 8 ends with Philip and Peter walking in the Holy Spirit as the gospel message moves to the ends of the earth. Luke continues documenting events in Acts 9 as he turns our attention to Saul. Saul was off to Damascus, and Jesus intervenes. He asks why Saul is persecuting him. This event catches Saul by surprise. Saul is overwhelmed with the evidence at this point and is called to share the faith of those he had been persecuting.

Saul Becomes Paul

Highlighting parts of this text:

Now Saul, <u>still breathing threats</u> and <u>murder</u> against <u>the disciples</u> of the Lord, went to the high priest, ² and asked for letters from him to the synagogues at Damascus, so that if he found any belonging to <u>the Way</u>, both men and women, he might bring them bound to Jerusalem. ³ As he was traveling, it happened that he was approaching Damascus, <u>*and suddenly a light from heaven flashed around him*</u>; ⁴ and he fell to the ground and heard <u>*a voice*</u> saying to him, "Saul, Saul, why are you persecuting Me?" ⁵ And he said, "Who are You, Lord?" And He *said*, "<u>*I am Jesus whom you are persecuting,*</u> ⁶ but get up and enter the city, and it will be told you what you must do." ⁷ The men who traveled with him stood speechless, hearing the voice but seeing no one. ⁸ Saul got up from the ground, and though his eyes were open, he could see nothing; and leading him by the hand, they brought him into Damascus. ⁹ And he was three days without sight, and neither ate nor drank.

¹⁰ Now there was a disciple at Damascus named Ananias; and <u>*the Lord said to him in a vision*</u>, "Ananias." And he said, "Here I am, Lord." ¹¹ And the Lord *said* to him, "Get up and go to the street called Straight, and inquire at the house of Judas for a man from Tarsus named Saul, for he is praying, ¹² and he has seen in <u>*a vision*</u> a man named Ananias come in and lay his hands on him, so that he might regain his sight." ¹³ But Ananias answered, "Lord, I have heard from many about this man, how much harm he did to Your saints at Jerusalem; ¹⁴ and here he has authority from the chief priests to bind all who call on Your name." ¹⁵ But the Lord said to him, "<u>*Go, for he is a chosen instrument of Mine, to bear My name before the Gentiles and kings and the sons of Israel*</u>; ¹⁶ <u>*for I will show him how much he must suffer for My name's sake.*</u>" ¹⁷ So Ananias departed and entered the house,

and after laying his hands on him said, "Brother Saul, the Lord Jesus, who appeared to you on the road by which you were coming, has sent me so that you may regain your sight and *be filled with the Holy Spirit*." ¹⁸ And immediately there fell from his eyes something like scales, and he regained his sight, and he got up and was *baptized*; ¹⁹ and he took food and was strengthened.

³¹ So the church throughout all Judea and Galilee and Samaria *enjoyed peace*, being built up; and going on in the fear of the Lord and *in the comfort of the Holy Spirit*, it continued to increase.

This provides the backstory for Saul. He was a relatively "bad dude" from the beginning. Jesus himself intervened. That's His choice to intervene. He's God and will do what he wishes. Some zealous Christians these days come across like they must motivate us to "convert" people, like Saul. I'm not suggesting we be silent, that's not my thinking here, but certainly the case is to begin with loving people and trust that the Holy Spirit will give us the words to speak and, more importantly, receptive minds, souls, and spirits to hear the great news expressed from joy, not under compulsion. Let's seek to walk in the Spirit and begin with a heart of love. It is this love that will shine in our relationships.

It is interesting that God felt it was important to tell Ananias that Paul was going to suffer. Remember, this is God. He reveals what He wishes, but for some reason He decided to give Ananias insight into the future. I can only imagine it was to ease Ananias's concerns, but there seems to be a strange "don't worry, he's going to get his" here.

Now, Saul is within the new faith. And here is a glimpse of God's plan. If Saul was a disciple from the beginning, his story and his ability to impact both Jews and eventually large portions of the Gentiles in the region might be less effective. What took place is a shock for the Jewish followers of Jesus.

They were faced with a man changed dramatically, not by their making of disciples of all nations, but once again, by the intervention of God through Jesus and the Holy Spirit. This appears to be the last direct intervention by Jesus himself. Throughout the remainder of Acts, we see the Holy Spirit becomes the person of the Trinity credited with most of the action.

Interventions With A Jew, Now A Gentile

I'll finish this section with observations from Acts 10.

> [10] Now *there was* a man at Caesarea named Cornelius, a centurion of what was called the Italian cohort, [2] a devout man and one who feared God with all his household and gave many alms to the *Jewish* people and prayed to God continually. [3] About the ninth hour of the day he clearly saw in a <u>*vision an angel of God*</u> who had *just* come in and said to him, "Cornelius!"

Once again, God acts with a vision, a vision of an angel. Cornelius is the first Gentile spoken of as the Holy Spirit is unleashed. God used Peter to bring the message to Cornelius. This is an early demonstration of the tension between Jews and Gentiles, which Paul will later be instrumental in changing. But what matters most is that God's at work. How about today?

Is not the Holy Spirit, God intervening each day? I read the next chapter. My views on evangelism are shaped by the fact that I see the focus as one of bringing the fullness of the Holy Spirit. This would be the key to impacting those around us. What hope do we have? Do people see our hope? Our fruit?

When I compare my reading with my past experiences, and observe a conflict between what I hear being taught and what I'm reading, I have difficulty resolving the two. Perhaps that's just my issue and no one else sees it, but I suspect it's because we are being overwhelmed by the agendas that we have embraced for hundreds of years.

I see the teaching supporting walking in the Spirit as the commandment. My preparation for this undertaking is to seek to understand God's power in every situation. Is it a process, or a personal relationship? The Great Relationship is a mystery.

It turns out that I may have surrounded myself with a subset of evangelical Christians that use terms like evangelism and Great Commission frequently. Not all Christians use this language, and therefore let me simply say, evangelism is portrayed as an activity that asks that we speak with everyone about the gospel or they might go to hell. That is a fairly good motivator. I mention that because thus far, there does not seem to be any action by people that was not directed by the living God, so when did God disappear and leave it up to us to go out on our own?

As for the Great Commission, that's the two verses, only two, from Matthew 28:19, 20, written after Paul nearly singlehandedly completed the "task." This has been the emphasis for so many for 100 to 150 years. I won't argue, but I say, go do your thing if you are called to do it.

Virtue Signaling

Thank goodness for 2015. British journalist James Bartholomew is often credited with originating the term "virtue signaling" in an article in *The Spectator* in 2015.[1]

Essentially, the meaning is to make a case for some action that others should be doing so as to be validated as a "virtuous" person. There's an element of shame in this process. Now that it was named, I recognized how often leaders in the church simply are "virtue signaling" as if their position would direct "all of us" to a virtuous outcome. This is the challenge with the "Vision Caster" model. And it elevates pastors, elders, overseers, whatever the title to a level of providing the actions we need to be doing.

In my estimation, we need to point out virtue signaling when it happens and then ask ourselves, is not our God greater? Is He not calling us to a Spiritu Ambulatio life?

Regarding the Great Commission, the message beyond those two verses is about a God that is alive today, and He calls each of us with our gifts to serve. It may not look like the way anyone expects. Let's set ourselves free to serve the power that God is providing through His Holy Spirit.

Black Slices And Loving Everyone Always

I was listening to messages from another church on the internet, and a presentation about loving everyone always was explained. It made sense, and my heart of contention was impacted. I wanted to adopt the "love everyone, always" principle.

---

[1] Bartholomew, James. "The awful rise of 'virtue signaling,'" *The Spectator*, April 18, 2015.

There are books on this subject. One is *Everybody, Always* from Bob Goff.[2] In essence, the question is: Why don't we love everyone, always? In order to answer this question, I came up with a visualization on how differences of opinion might be handled or visualized. I have used it to see interpersonal situations differently. I don't always utilize this effectively, but I make an effort. I call my visualization "black slices."

R. C. Sproul is a theologian and recorded a series called, "Renewing Your Mind." The image that comes to mind with R. C. Sproul is a type of "blue collar" theologian. I do not analyze every thought or opinion he has, but they seemed to make sense. One day, he brought up the concept called the noetic effects of sin. All of our minds are impacted by incorrect thoughts, ideas, and beliefs. We may have many of the right beliefs, but we are prone to distorted thoughts and ideas. This is common to all of us. We may make different errors, but we all make them. Thus, the black slices. Imagine a circle that can be partitioned in slices, which are larger or smaller and can be placed in different positions.

---

2 Goff, Bob. *Everybody, Always.* Nashville: Nelson Books, 2018.

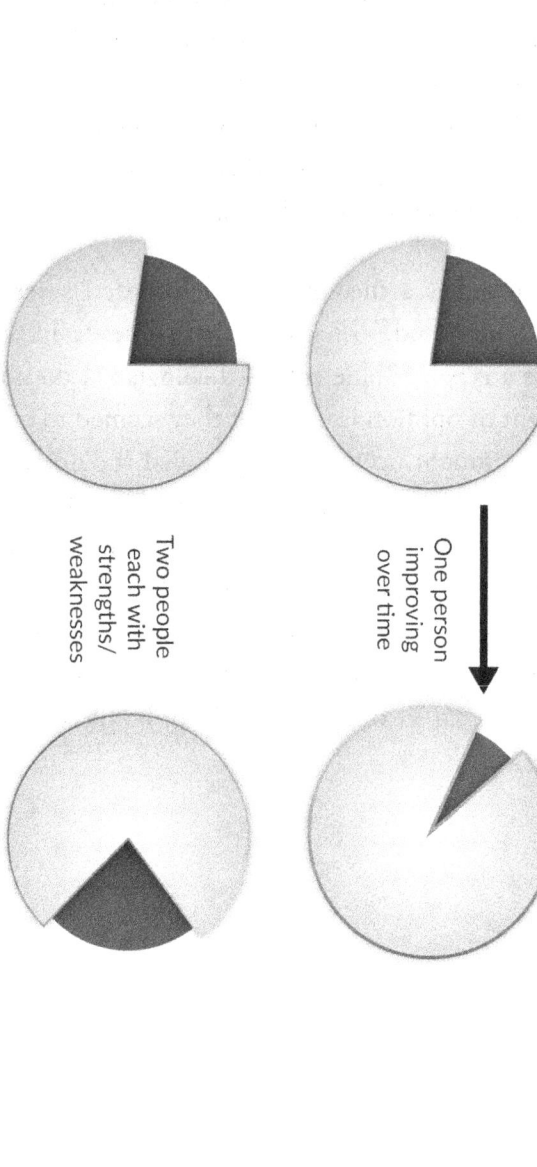

The "black slice" represents our noetic effects of sin, none of us are perfect, and our imperfections show up in different areas, such as pride, personal discipline, communications, beliefs, even opinions that mix into being more important than perhaps they should be.

One person improving over time

Two people each with strengths/ weaknesses

Two people with different "weaknesses" may recognize the weaknesses in others easier. A challenge will be if the two people are supportive and will work with the other person to understand the other's view, or be dismissive and stubborn that they are correct.

Each circle represents a person. Each of us has a slice or multiple slices that simply are filled in black, representing ideas we may have that are likely off from what God ideally calls us to think. Our conflicts, even between people of faith, may result from one person having clarity on thoughts, beliefs, or ideas that would be a blind spot or a black slice for someone else.

Additionally, in organizations, groupthink aligns the black slices so that all those in the group begin to experience conformity in their thoughts and make agreements amongst themselves about how the group should believe, think, and behave. Then conflict arises when someone challenges the accepted norms.

Well, one of my strengths is inclusion; I'm an includer. Welcome, reader, I'm including you! One description of this strength is that the includer is instinctively more sensitive than most people to what it feels like to be left out of a group, a conversation, or an activity. One of my frustrations with my Lutheran upbringing was I felt left out, disconnected from the community. There were several reasons for it. My father was absent, and the church was farther away from our home. As a result, no one from my school was in attendance. So, it was isolating.

The Includer

I prefer to include everyone. And because I wasn't enamored with this denominational thing, I felt left out while some jumped on this new pastor's bandwagon. I don't like "in or out" thinking.

My own blind spot (black slice) came out. Even though I cast few judgments, I criticized those who belonged to exclusive groups and clubs. While I disagreed with what they stood for and may have viewed them as elitist, I didn't remember that everyone has the right to choose the people with whom they spend time. That's perfectly okay in typical social situations, but my expectations for the church were high, and in hindsight perhaps too high.

How to resolve this was not clear.

I felt like an outsider in this group. I kept up my daily reading and journaling. I repeated the process every four months, hoping to increase the fruit of the Spirit in my life: love, joy, peace, patience, kindness, goodness, faithfulness, gentleness, self-control. All the same, my black slice was coming out.

My naming myself an "includer" comes from input from Gallup's CliftonStrengths assessment.[3] One answers several situational questions and a profile is formed. One of my top 5 of 34 is Includer. My weakest strength is Harmony. That puzzles me, but then I combined that with my includer concept. I actually want to include everyone, but that doesn't mean I have an expectation that everyone agrees on every opinion.

But as I consider this dilemma, a light went off. I come across as contentious and contrarian with leaders of these religious groups when they take exclusive positions. If they don't take exclusive positions, then everyone will be included, but if leadership declares someone is a false teacher, well that is going to exclude those who may not agree, or worse, not find it important at all. There's a recommendation to invest in self-awareness.

---

3 Gallup CliftonStrengths Assessment. Retrieved from: https://www.gallup.com/cliftonstrengths/en/252137/home.aspx

Not Understood

My contrarian, contentious behavior towards a small number of people is not good, but it was limited, at least! I thought that others had their own black slice. And in this framework, my black slice might be oriented in a different part of the circle than the black slices of others. With this framework, I could consider that others are likely very different from me in personality, type, and had different strengths and gifts. Certainly, I have been reading about spiritual gifts over and over in Paul's letters, chapter by chapter, month by month.

My choice, even though it is not perfected, is to love all people. The fact that an entire denominational leadership can make announcements about other pastors as false teachers and share that common belief yet be blind to their own false teaching is amazing. I never wanted that to be the case, but it is. And to keep sane, I simply say these folks all have their black slices.

This is the situation where a group has the same incorrect thinking or behavior and yet they don't realize it unless they listen to someone who clearly sees their black slice, since theirs are all positioned in the same way.

The Sixth Sola

Here is the challenge with many denominations: The organization has agreed to align themselves over certain beliefs. They may not be accounting for others' views, but the organization is not interested in inclusion, but are more interested in harmony and being correct, so it sets up conflict that they don't recognize because the leadership all share the same "bad idea" or even incorrect belief. Those that see the issue clearly, for whatever reason, are excluded from discussion, because it would require the "groupthink" to make too many changes.

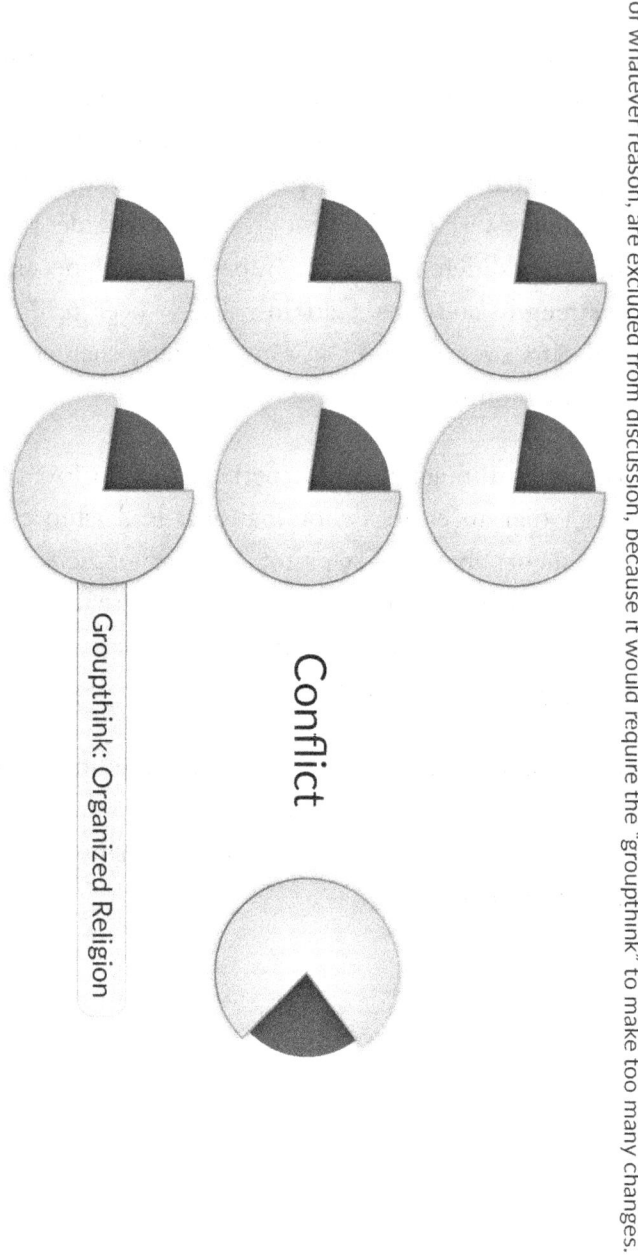

Groupthink: Organized Religion

Conflict

72

None of us are 100 percent clean in thought or behavior, so we all tend to be defensive and find the black slice in the other person. It's there, I have them too, but I don't have a black slice positioned where many others have them.

During this time of daily reading, chapter by chapter, my faith and convictions have been strengthened. When an elder called me out with verses plucked from 1 Timothy, 2 Timothy, 2 Thessalonians, and other places, I listen, but then verify. It turns out, upon further review, the criticism directed my way was out of line.

False Teacher Or False Bretheran?

That's the elder's black slice. He has an agenda, he is convinced he is right, and drops truth on me. If I hadn't had years now of studying these same passages, in context, I would crumble under the "authority" of an elder. But I'm not doing that. Those verses that he thinks apply to me do not. But there's no arguing over it. It can be lonely to walk in the Spirit, as others don't seem to understand.

I can love these people. It's their black slice. I want to go with the love everyone always position, and this black slice framework helps me do it. Typically, I have to win the argument. Now, I can move on more often. It's an ongoing process and part of my transformation.

This framework should be useful. Let's consider other's shortcomings, black slices and yet affirm that we can love those we struggle to love. In businesses, I would say this is similar to grace. In the end, it all starts with understanding the message

God has given us. And it's not just a message of words, but also His Holy Spirit.

Next, we keep moving with what Luke is describing with these earlier followers of Jesus after His Ascension and sending of His Holy Spirit.

CHAPTER 6

THE VIQ: "DID YOU RECEIVE THE HOLY SPIRIT WHEN YOU BELIEVED?": ACTS 11–19

The question of this chapter: "Did you receive the Holy Spirit when you believed?" is what I call the VIQ or "very important question." In order to dive into the meaning and significance of this question, I would like to take us there from chapters 11 to 19. God, His Holy Spirit, His angels are intervening with many types of people in various places every step of the way. It all comes to an interesting conclusion in chapter 19.

Acts 11, Peter returns to Jerusalem and the debate begins about Jews and Gentiles. In the 21st century, I would venture that many of us do not consider the distinction between Jew and Gentile. As Gentile Christians, we may easily overlook the beginning of what was a Jewish faith. We may consider this old news or take a fresh look at what occurred.

Peter explains in Acts 11:

> ¹³ And he reported to us how he had seen _the angel_ standing in his house, and saying, "Send to Joppa and have Simon, who is also called Peter, brought here; ¹⁴ and he will speak words to you by which you will be saved, you and all your household." ¹⁵ And as I began to speak, _the Holy Spirit_ fell upon them just as _He did_ upon us at the beginning. ¹⁶ And _I remembered_ the word of the Lord, how He used to say, "_John baptized with water, but you will be baptized with the Holy Spirit_. ¹⁷ Therefore if God gave to them _the same gift_ as _He gave_ to us also _after believing_ in the Lord Jesus Christ, who was I that I could stand in God's way?" ¹⁸ When they heard this, they quieted down and glorified God, saying, "_Well then, God has granted to the Gentiles also the repentance that leads to life_."

You are likely familiar with these passages. I ask that we don't read over them so quickly and possibly miss the intervention of the Holy Spirit. The Jews are cautious. They hesitate to consider the broader implications of the significance of Jesus's death, Resurrection, Ascension, and the coming of the Holy Spirit. They have resistance and are under pressure from those in the Jewish faith and Jewish traditions. And now, God intervenes to bring the message of what he has done for the people that were outsiders, the Gentiles.

> ²⁰ But there were some of them, men of Cyprus and Cyrene, who came to Antioch and _began_ speaking to the Greeks also, preaching the Lord Jesus. ²¹ And _the hand of the Lord_ was with them, and a large number who believed turned to the Lord. ²² The news about them reached the ears of the church

at Jerusalem, and they sent Barnabas off to Antioch. ²³ Then when he arrived and witnessed the grace of God, he rejoiced and *began* to encourage them all with resolute heart to remain *true* to the Lord; ²⁴ for he was a good man, and <u>*full of the Holy Spirit*</u> and of faith. And considerable numbers were brought to the Lord. ²⁵ And he left for Tarsus to <u>*look for Saul*</u>; ²⁶ and when he had found him, he brought him to Antioch. And for <u>*an entire year*</u> they met with the church and taught considerable numbers; and <u>*the disciples*</u> were first called <u>*Christians*</u> in Antioch.

Today, we often read this with a sense of, "If only we could do that!" This is true of those of us with a zeal for missions and a zeal to make an impact for Jesus. This is the excitement we may express to ourselves, thinking we can influence each other to really "do it this time." Can you imagine the impact we could have for God?

We may not realize that we are doing this, but we may be enamored with the results that come out of our efforts. And yet can we see that it is not Peter, Barnabas, or Saul? It is God.

Who Is Influencing Whom?

The message of God continues; it is the "hand of the Lord" that is influential in these events. Barnabas was full of the Holy Spirit. This is not a casual statement. Luke describes him this way because it is important. We may want to pause over these words as if we were reading them for the first time. When we notice the language with which Luke is writing, we can see that he's demonstrating an important and consistent pattern in the movement of God.

Barnabas calls on Saul and brings him to teach with him. They remained for a year teaching Gentiles and perhaps Jews as well. Luke points out that the disciples were first called Christians. In the last 50 years or so of American Christianity, there's been a movement to form discipleship groups. The message that it sends is there is a program one can follow to become an "elite Christian." Yet this passage debunks that thought. If we have faith, we are disciples. Based on many of the statements of Luke, they were disciples before they were even Christians.

In Acts 12, Peter is back. This time, Herod the king arrests Peter after having James the brother of John killed by the sword. Attacks on those following this faith were coming from Jewish spiritual leaders and now the Jewish political leader as well.

God intervenes,

> ⁷ And behold, <u>an angel of the Lord</u> suddenly appeared and a light shone in the cell; and <u>he struck</u> Peter's side and woke him up, saying, "<u>Get up quickly</u>." And his chains fell off his hands. ⁸ And the angel said to him, "<u>Gird yourself and put on your sandals</u>." And he did so. And he * said to him, "<u>Wrap your cloak around you and follow me</u>."

Peter is led out of prison. God takes action. The same circumstances may not occur today, but do we consider that God may be just as active if we are in an emotional prison, an economic prison, a spiritual prison? Again, each of us has our challenges to overcome, and here's Scripture describing how God intervenes. Reading this encourages me to pray for God's intervention. He has done it before, and even today we continue to see the actions of the living God.

Even as I edit this portion, reminders come my way. I read of this angel striking Peter. I believe God would do this today if He desired. I don't know many people in the 21st century who are having this experience. Even so, perhaps there are people being struck. Luke recorded this event as it occurred. He must have spoken with Peter. Can you imagine Peter meeting Luke: "So Peter, what has been your experience? How has God been speaking to you in your quiet time?" Peter might answer, "Well, I don't know about my 'quiet time,' but I was getting hit to wake up by an angel of God, and he was treating me like a kid, telling me to put on my coat. So that's kind of been my experience."

Notice it is not Jesus who is telling Peter to follow him. It is a spiritual being. This is what is different from the gospel of John. That period is gone forever, so we move forward.

The excitement continues at the end of Acts 12 with the end of Herod and the movement of Barnabas and Saul.

> 21 On an appointed day Herod, having put on his royal apparel, took his seat on the rostrum and *began* delivering an address to them. 22 The people kept crying out, "The voice of a god and not of a man!" 23 And immediately <u>an angel of the Lord struck him</u> because he did not give God the glory, and he was eaten by worms and died.
>
> 24 But the word of the Lord continued to grow and to be multiplied.
>
> 25 And Barnabas and Saul returned from Jerusalem when they had fulfilled their mission, taking along with *them* John, who was also called Mark.

The Lord intervened again, striking Herod down this time. The message is clear: God can do anything and His will is not deterred by humans.

Acts 13 begins with the preparation for the first missionary journey.

> ² While they were ministering to the Lord and fasting, <u>the Holy Spirit</u> said, "<u>Set apart for Me Barnabas and Saul for the work to which I have called them</u>." ³ Then, when they had fasted and prayed and laid their hands on them, they sent them away.

> ⁴ So, being sent out by <u>the Holy Spirit</u>, they went down to Seleucia and from there they sailed to Cyprus.

Saul is empowered once again by the Holy Spirit to speak words against a magician that was thwarting the message for Barnabas and Saul, and here is when Luke references him as Paul.

> ⁹ But Saul, who was <u>also known as Paul</u>, filled with <u>the Holy Spirit</u>, fixed his gaze on him, ¹⁰ and said, "You who are full of all deceit and fraud, you son of the devil, you enemy of all righteousness, will you not cease to make crooked the straight ways of the Lord?"

Paul speaks with the authority of the Holy Spirit. Do we have the same Holy Spirit in our lives? Do you have something to say? It may only be to your closest family and friends, but you do have something to say.

At the end of Acts 13, Paul speaks to the Jews in the synagogue. There was eager response, and they were encouraged to return the next week. Yet the leaders of the Jewish people were jealous of the influence Paul and Barnabas had with the people, so they worked against them.

> ⁴⁵ But when the Jews saw the crowds, they were <u>filled with jealousy</u> and *began* contradicting the things spoken by Paul and were blaspheming. ⁴⁶ Paul and Barnabas <u>*spoke out boldly*</u> and said, "It was necessary that the Word of God be spoken to you first; since you repudiate it and <u>*judge yourselves unworthy of eternal life*</u>, behold, we are turning to the Gentiles. ⁴⁷ For so the Lord has commanded us,
>
> 'I have placed You as a light for the Gentiles,
> That You may bring salvation to the end of the earth.'"
>
> ⁴⁸ When <u>*the Gentiles*</u> heard this, they *began* rejoicing and glorifying the word of the Lord; and <u>*as many as had been appointed to eternal life believed*</u>. ⁴⁹ And the word of the Lord was being spread through the whole region. ⁵⁰ But the Jews incited the devout women of prominence and the leading men of the city, and instigated a persecution against Paul and Barnabas, and drove them out of their district. ⁵¹ But they shook off the dust of their feet *in protest* against them and went to Iconium. ⁵² And the <u>disciples</u> were <u>*continually filled with joy and with the Holy Spirit*</u>.

Do We Prefer To Be Led?

Here is the battle between the established religion of its time and this new message. Enough of the leaders were embittered to work against them, and viewing the situation purely from the human element, the Jews were losing whatever power they had over their followers. They wanted to stop this movement of the Holy Spirit that was flowing through Paul and Barnabas.

Again, we have immediate disciples. Some would say they were made by the Holy Spirit, by the preaching, and as it says, they were filled with joy and the Holy Spirit. To say, as some do, that disciples are made, not born, is to overlook that there is no program or human making that brings discipleship. It is only the Holy Spirit working in the hearts of people. Too often the message is that by trying harder, by memorizing more verses, by being compliant to a system, then and only then true discipleship occurs. But it is simply Spiritu Ambulatio.

Later we will see Paul describing the fruit of the Spirit, one of which is joy. It is quite prominent in those witnessing the events recorded by Luke. Remember, Luke is often asking questions of the people that were there and these are the words and expressions that were *remembered*. Think about some amazing experience you had 10 years ago. Do you remember every detail? Likely not, but you do remember how you felt and the impression with which it left you. Luke is capturing those words for us.

Remember, Luke is a human being. I don't see evidence that he has joined Paul at this point, so it is likely Luke recording what Paul later told him. I mention this not to create any controversy but to remind us that there is a person behind the telling of these events.

The Jews And Gentiles

Next, in Acts 14 a pattern continues. They arrive at a new city and speak in the synagogue. Paul and Barnabas are approaching "their people." They know the culture and the practices. Naturally, they head into the synagogue and know that they are going to see resistance.

> ² But the Jews who disbelieved stirred up the minds of the Gentiles and embittered them against the brethren. ³ Therefore, they spent <u>a long time</u> there speaking <u>boldly with reliance upon the Lord</u>, <u>who</u> was testifying to the word of <u>His grace</u>, granting that signs and wonders be done by their hands.

This is not to say that any of us should desire to be in this exact position, nor that we *should* do anything based on these events. Instead, perhaps in the challenges you face you may consider taking hold of the encouragement that the Lord is present. We may not see him at work, but this is evidence.

In the remainder of Acts 14, Paul is stoned and survives. Barnabas and Paul continue forward and return to the beginning of this first missionary journey.

> ²⁷ When they had arrived and gathered the church together, they *began* to report all things that <u>God had done</u> with them and how He had opened a door of *faith to the Gentiles*. ²⁸ And they spent a long time with the disciples.

Here, Luke says again that it is God who does. The message is that the Gentiles can enter into the calling that was first given to Abraham. Paul will discuss in several of his letters that the promise of the Great Relationship was first given to Abraham. Let's walk in it.

Acts 15, the Jew versus Gentile debate continues. We now see the specific issue of circumcision addressed. This physical sign on the body of every Jew was symbolic of the covenant God made with the Jews. If Jesus is to continue the Jewish traditions, then perhaps circumcision should be a requirement for Gentile converts.

> ¹⁵ Some men came down from Judea and *began* teaching the brethren, "Unless you are _circumcised_ according to the custom of Moses, you cannot be saved."

The meeting in Jerusalem is significant, with Peter making a conclusive statement.

> ⁶ The apostles and the elders came together to look into this matter. ⁷ After there had been _much debate_, Peter stood up and said to them, "Brethren, you know that in the early days God made a choice among you, that by my mouth the Gentiles would hear the word of the gospel and believe. ⁸ And God, who knows the heart, testified to them _giving them the Holy Spirit_, just as He also did to us; ⁹ and He made _no distinction_ between us and them, _cleansing their hearts by faith_. ¹⁰ Now therefore why do you put God to the test by placing upon the neck of the disciples a yoke which neither our fathers nor we have been able to bear? ¹¹ But we believe that _we are saved_ through _the grace of the Lord Jesus_, in the same way as they also are."

An initial observation is that debate was accepted. Do you ever run into situations where you do not believe you are being heard? Some would rather ignore questions and challenges than really listen, understand, and communicate that they understood the message. When Luke uses the words, "much debate," I imagine a strenuous discussion. God is the one moving, not just the message, but also His actual Holy Spirit to Gentiles amidst these early doctrinal tensions.

Peter's point is that the Gentiles received the Holy Spirit. The evidence is a cleansed heart by their professions of faith in the proclaimed message. He notes that the Gentiles *and* even the Jews are saved through the same grace. This debate will continue for years to come. Do we commit to outward works (in this case, circumcision), or are we in a relationship with God by His grace alone? Sola Gratia to bring in a Sola!

The summary statement of all the debate took the form of a letter to the Gentile believers that responded to the Holy Spirit's call to faith.

> [27] Therefore we have sent Judas and Silas, who themselves will *also report* the same things by word *of mouth*. [28] "For it seemed good to *the Holy Spirit* and to us to lay upon you no greater burden than these essentials: [29] that you abstain from things sacrificed to idols and from blood and from things strangled and from fornication; if you keep yourselves free from such things, you will do well. Farewell."

The group decided to send Judas and Silas to report. This gives credence to Paul's and Barnabas's thoughts that they should not be circumcised. That's an amazing simplified instruction considering these Jews had a lengthy list of things to do and not to do under their previous religious orders. And once again, the Holy Spirit is integral to all these events.

Okay To Agree To Disagree?

At the end of Acts 15, there was a disagreement between Paul and Barnabas, and the next missionary journey in Acts 16 was a disagreement between Paul and Silas without Barnabas. The message here may be that we can have our differences and yet share the same faith, the same God, the same Holy Spirit. The outworking of this event is what comes next. Some ask, who was right? Barnabas or Paul? It probably doesn't matter, but we do know that Barnabas never wrote anything that made it into the New Testament, if that's any indication.

Acts 16 starts with the introduction of Timothy into the history of the early church. Timothy will be a longtime companion of Paul's throughout the remainder of Paul's life. We have an odd occurrence based on what we just witnessed with the conclusion of the Gentile and circumcision discussion.

> ¹⁶ Paul came also to Derbe and to Lystra. And <u>*a disciple*</u> was there, named <u>*Timothy*</u>, the son of <u>*a Jewish woman*</u> who was <u>a believer</u>, but his father was a Greek, ² and he was well spoken of by the brethren who were in Lystra and Iconium. ³ Paul wanted this man to go with him; and he took him and <u>*circumcised him*</u> because of <u>*the Jews*</u> who were in those parts, for they all knew that his father was a Greek.

This circumcision is puzzling, yet it may be the mixture of Timothy's mother's Jewish nature. Note, she's a believer, and I would say that based on what we have read, she is filled with the Holy Spirit. Paul appears to be concerned about "the Jews." Is it important? If it is, I would expect to read more about it, and if not, I'm prepared to let this go. What is clear is that when it comes to where Paul would be going, it was the Holy Spirit guiding the way forward.

> [6] They passed through the Phrygian and Galatian region, having *been forbidden* by *the Holy Spirit* to speak the word in Asia; [7] and after they came to Mysia, they were trying to go into Bithynia, and *the Spirit of Jesus* did not permit them; [8] and passing by Mysia, they came down to Troas. [9] A vision appeared to Paul in the night.

Is God Finished Intervening?

Are you forbidden by the Holy Spirit to speak? Paul was on the move. He was seeking to serve and follow his calling to bring this message to Gentiles and he could go in many directions. Could it be that the Holy Spirit is intervening when we are moving? And what does moving mean in your situation?

> And then a vision appeared…God is once again intervening.

> [10] When he had seen *the vision*, immediately we sought to go into Macedonia, concluding that God had called us to preach the gospel to them.

> [11] So putting out to sea from Troas, we ran a straight course to Samothrace, and on the day following to Neapolis; [12] and from there to *Philippi*, which is a leading city of the district of Macedonia, a *Roman* colony; and we were staying in this city for some days.

Paul is called into Macedonia, northern Greece today, and to the city of Philippi in particular. He followed a practice of speaking to Jews then Gentiles. Later, Paul wrote a letter to the Philippians. It was after many other events, and though we see his stay was brief, Paul would have continued to hear of the events happening in this city.

When Paul and Silas spoke, there was response. They were even followed by a fortune-teller that understood what they were saying and yet annoyed Paul to the point of frustration. Paul commanded the spirit to leave, and the fortune-teller lost her powers.

Those that made money from this fortune-teller had Paul and Silas put in prison. Then God acts once again to free them from their condition.

> ²⁵ But about midnight Paul and Silas were praying and singing hymns of praise to God, and the prisoners were listening to them; ²⁶ *and suddenly* there came *a great earthquake*, so that the foundations of the prison house were shaken; and immediately all the doors were opened and everyone's chains were unfastened.

God acts "suddenly," only this time it is not with an angel intervening, but with an earthquake. This earthquake is attributed to the actions of God, though it may appear as a normal event. They are out of prison and are told to move on. They do, as we read in Acts 17.

> ¹⁷ Now when they had traveled through Amphipolis and Apollonia, they came to *Thessalonica*, where there was a

synagogue of the Jews. ² And according to Paul's custom, he went to them, and for three Sabbaths *reasoned with them* from the Scriptures, ³ explaining and giving evidence that the Christ had to suffer and rise again from the dead, and *saying,* "*This Jesus whom I am proclaiming to you is the Christ.*"

Paul On The Move

Paul has come out of Galatia and into Macedonia. Now we see him in Thessalonica. This is new territory, new customs and culture, yet Paul faces similar opposition. Luke is recording the events. What message is he sending us? I imagine we have all heard the quotation in Acts 17:6–8. But what is the context? What was going on?

> ⁶ When they did not find them, they began dragging Jason and some brethren before the city authorities, shouting, "These men who have upset the world have come here also; ⁷ and Jason has welcomed them, and they all act contrary to the decrees of Caesar, saying that there is another king, Jesus." ⁸ They stirred up the crowd and the city authorities who heard these things.

> ¹⁰ The brethren immediately sent Paul and Silas away by night to Berea, and when they arrived, they went into the synagogue of the Jews.

Now they are off to Berea, a neighboring city. And the heat continues to be turned up on Paul and Silas. Those upset in Thessalonica came after them in Berea. Persistent buggers.

¹⁴ Then immediately the brethren sent Paul out to go as far as the sea; and Silas and Timothy remained there. ¹⁵ Now those who escorted Paul brought him as far *as Athens*; and receiving a command for Silas and Timothy to come to him as soon as possible, they left.

Paul is hanging out in Athens, the most populated city in Greece, because he's getting chased out of the other areas. This was not Paul's plan, yet I would say he's still walking in the Spirit and following where the Lord is leading him. Here, he is invited to make comments to the city's philosophical audience. This is one of my personal favorite events that Paul engages in.

¹⁶ Now while Paul was waiting for them at Athens, *his spirit* was being provoked within him as he was observing the city full of idols. ¹⁷ So he was *reasoning* in the synagogue with the Jews and the God-fearing *Gentiles*, and in the marketplace every day with those who happened to be present. ¹⁸ And also some of *the Epicurean and Stoic philosophers* were conversing with him. Some were saying, "What would this *idle babbler* wish to say?" Others, "He seems to be a *proclaimer of strange deities*,"—because he was preaching Jesus and the Resurrection. ¹⁹ And they took him and brought him to *the Areopagus*, saying, "May we know what this new teaching is which you are proclaiming? ²⁰ For you are bringing some strange things to our ears; so we want to know what these things mean." ²¹ (Now all the Athenians and the strangers visiting there used to *spend their time in nothing other than telling or hearing something new*.)

This is fantastic! One, we see Paul sensitive to his spirit. And he is reasoning and overheard by philosophers who then invite him to the Areopagus. And the description of this place always has me in laughter: "spend their time in nothing other than telling or hearing something new." Amazing.

No Jesus?

Luke continues with the words spoken by Paul to this audience.

> ²² So Paul stood in the midst of the <u>Areopagus</u> and said, "Men of Athens, I observe that you are <u>very religious in all respects</u>. ²³ For while I was passing through and examining the objects of your worship, I also found an altar with this inscription, 'TO AN UNKNOWN GOD.' Therefore what <u>you worship in ignorance</u>, this I proclaim to you. ²⁴ The God who made the world and all things in it, since He is Lord of heaven and earth, <u>does not dwell in temples made with hands</u>; ²⁵ nor is He served by human hands, as though He needed anything, since He Himself <u>gives to all people life and breath and all things</u>; ²⁶ and He made from one *man* every nation of mankind to live on all the face of the earth, having determined *their* appointed times and the boundaries of their habitation, ²⁷ that they would <u>seek God</u>, if perhaps they might grope for Him and find Him, though <u>He is not far from each one of us</u>; ²⁸ for in Him we live and move and exist, as even some of your own poets have said, '<u>For we also are His children</u>.' ²⁹ <u>Being then the children of God</u>, we ought not to think that the Divine Nature is like gold or silver or stone, <u>an image formed by the art and thought of man</u>. ³⁰ Therefore having <u>overlooked the times of ignorance</u>, God is now <u>declaring</u>

to men that *all people* everywhere should repent, ³¹ because He has fixed a day in which He will judge the world in righteousness *through a Man* whom He has appointed, having furnished proof to all men by *raising Him from the dead*."

Paul communicates with a Greek philosophical mindset. The highlighting of words brings the salient points home. Let's look at how this unfolds.

- He acknowledges they are religious.
- They have an UNKNOWN GOD, and he declares they worship in ignorance.
- He tells them he will explain this God that is unknown.
- God does not dwell in temples made by man.
- Our existence is from this God.
- Some give up and ignore the signs of his existence, others still seek.
- He is not far from each of us.
- Paul does not argue with their claims that they are children of God.
- A reminder: Man does not make God from art or thoughts.

And Paul moves into what has changed:

- God overlooks our ignorance.
- He declares to all people now, not just Jews.
- He declares through a man (he doesn't name Jesus).
- The important thing about "this man" is that he's been raised from the dead.

Paul speaks to them from their viewpoint. He's entered into their culture and comments on what he's learned about them before he speaks of his culture and experience. He doesn't even use Jewish terms or history. There is not one mention, and interestingly enough, he doesn't even use the name of Jesus. This presentation has an impact on the listeners. Paul then moves on to Corinth.

On To Corinth

Acts 18 continues:

> ¹⁸ After these things he left Athens and went to Corinth. ² And he found a Jew named <u>Aquila</u>, a native of Pontus, having recently come from Italy with his wife <u>Priscilla</u>, because Claudius had commanded all the Jews to leave Rome.
>
> ⁹ And <u>the Lord said to Paul</u> in the night <u>by a vision</u>, "Do not be afraid *any longer*, but go on speaking and do not be silent; ¹⁰ for I am with you, and no man will attack you in order to harm you, for *I have many people* in this city." ¹¹ And he settled *there* a year and six months, <u>teaching the Word of God</u> among them.

Luke records why Aquila and Priscilla came from Rome and are now in Corinth. They were Jews removed from Rome, likely because they were believers in the new covenant. It doesn't say here that Paul spoke to them about Jesus, the gospel, or the Holy Spirit, and then they became believers. By this time, the message is spreading throughout the Roman Empire. It's noteworthy that God says He has "many people" in the city.

¹⁸ Paul, having remained many days longer, took leave of the brethren and put out to sea for Syria, and with him were *Priscilla* and *Aquila*.

These two are joining Paul. We don't know why Luke is mentioning them at this time, but much like Stephen was mentioned in Acts 6, it is not to teach us not to complain but simply to let us know how Stephen became involved in the church at that time. Here, Priscilla and Aquila had a relationship with Paul that was endearing. We don't know exactly why, but it could be because they worked together or that they were Jews that had faith in the new covenant because of what God had done.

¹⁹ They came to Ephesus, and he left them there.

Paul leaves Priscilla and Aquila in Ephesus. Remember, we are not reading unconnected verses that are to be pulled out for instruction. There's a reason for this background information, and we are about to hit the punchline.

²⁴ Now a Jew named *Apollos*, an Alexandrian by birth, *an eloquent man*, came to Ephesus; and he was *mighty in the Scriptures*. ²⁵ This man had been instructed in the way of the Lord; and being *fervent in spirit*, he was speaking and *teaching accurately the things concerning Jesus*, being acquainted *only* with *the baptism of John*; ²⁶ and he began to speak out boldly in the synagogue. But when *Priscilla* and *Aquila* heard him, they *took him aside* and explained to him *the way of God more accurately*.

And what do we learn about Apollos? He's:

The VIQ: "Did You Receive the Holy Spirit When You Believed?": Acts 11–19

- Eloquent
- Mighty in the Scriptures
- Fervent in spirit
- Teaching accurately the things concerning Jesus
- Only acquainted with the baptism of John

What happens next?

Consider This

Priscilla and Aquila take him aside and explain to him the way of God more accurately. And what does that mean? We don't exactly find out until the next chapter, yet we know that it's possible to "not fully understand the way of God." Apollos is by all external evidence a charismatic leader for the gospel of Jesus. But what is missing? We turn the page to Acts 19.

> ¹⁹ It happened that while Apollos was at Corinth, <u>*Paul*</u> passed through the upper country and came to Ephesus and found some <u>*disciples*</u>. ² He said to them, "<u>*Did you receive the Holy Spirit when you believed?*</u>" And they *said* to him, "<u>*No*</u>, we have not even heard whether <u>*there is a Holy Spirit*</u>." ³ And he said, "<u>*Into what then were you baptized?*</u>" And they said, "<u>*Into John's baptism.*</u>" ⁴ Paul said, "<u>*John baptized with the baptism of repentance, telling the people to believe in Him who was coming after him, that is, in Jesus.*</u>" ⁵ When they heard this, they were baptized in the name of the Lord Jesus. ⁶ And when Paul had laid his hands upon them, <u>*the Holy Spirit*</u> came on them, and they *began speaking* with tongues and *prophesying*. ⁷ There were in all about 12 men.

This is a clear discussion of what Apollos is missing. He is missing the Holy Spirit. I purposely have walked through these chapters to show how reading a chapter a day gives context. There is a message I may miss if I only read two or three verses, memorize them, and pull them out for some specific case. Why not get the entire message? This is all plain language. I don't see any reason to complicate further what we have with deep-dive analysis.

Luke records that it is possible to teach accurately about Jesus, to preach the gospel, to get all the theological facts correct, and yet still miss the essential truth of the Holy Spirit. This is Luke, describing what took place. It seems logical to ask whether this still happens today. I don't see anything in the remaining Scriptures to suggest that this is unique to that time. This is actually my story. I didn't recognize it for many years, but when I came to this section of Scripture, it dawned on me that this is what I experience. I analyzed and yet that did not bring the understanding. I might have been an Apollos, and I might be with many "Apollos" leaders that teach accurately but not be moved by the Holy Spirit. However, God intervened, nearly 40 years ago.

This raises the question for each of us to consider. If I am asked about receiving the Holy Spirit, I would answer yes. I didn't "speak in tongues" or "prophesy" but I can't explain how I could sit in church, hear the gospel over and over, quite possibly be taught accurately, but never understand the message. If my family situation was different, I might have stuck with accurate teaching about Jesus without receiving the Spirit.

Now I have confidence in what Jesus describes to Nicodemus in the Gospel of John about being born again. I say, yes, that's it. I have faith and believe, and it has to be the Holy Spirit that caused that rebirth. That's my experience, my thinking, my position.

How Do You Answer?

It is likely that if you have read this far that you at least respect the teachings of Christianity. You may attend a church and have knowledge of the events behind the faith. But here, Paul asks the question, "Did you receive the Holy Spirit when you believed?" That's a question only you can answer. It could open up a time of reflection. If you answer yes, I have received the Holy Spirit, then that may be your reason for confidence in your faith, your calling, your mission.

The question brings me to reflect on my experience with a person who expressed a changed attitude, mindset, and outwardly demonstrated the fruit of the Spirit in joy, peace, and kindness. They helped me to acknowledge that it is from God. He is my connection to receiving the Holy Spirit. I understood for the first time, over 40 years ago, that I'd missed the Spirit with the emphasis I was placing on accuracy.

It's possible for the most eloquent church leaders to teach accurately about Jesus without the fullness of the Holy Spirit. The timing of this book coincided with my local church teaching on the "Unleashing of the Gospel" as the theme for the Book of Acts. I felt from the beginning that it would be better described as the "Unleashing of the Holy Spirit."

Lo and behold, these verses were overlooked.

This is not an argument one way or another. It's my observation. We could dig into commentaries and surely many respected people have an opinion, but if the Scriptures are inerrant and inspired by God, there can be plenty of accuracy about Jesus and not enough about the Holy Spirit.

Why The Apparent Avoidance Of The Holy Spirit?

This is my passion for the Sola Spiritu Ambulatio. I want to understand this Holy Spirit and not just intellectually. It is a sanctification and a growth mindset for me. It may have been difficult to walk through these chapters, but I wanted to demonstrate the flow of events. I didn't want to pull out Acts 19:2 and parade it around without setting the context. What we see in the flow of passages are continuous actions from God, the Holy Spirit, and His angels. There's a reason why Luke presents these events, and I suggest that it's because it is what happened. This is significant for us and for how we approach our days. I believe this is my calling from the Spirit and so my hope is to name a few things and see if others resonate.

What is the overall message of the passages we've been reading? Luke has brought us this far. Paul is in Ephesus and plans to go to Rome. There is value in connecting the movements of Paul, Peter, John, but most importantly, seeing them in light of how the Holy Spirit is moving them.

Paul's question is one we may struggle with. That's the challenge from this book. How do we know if we received the Holy Spirit? There's more ahead, and for completeness, let's see if we have any information from the remainder of the book of Acts in 19 to 28.

CHAPTER 7

STILL IN JAIL AFTER ALL THESE YEARS, ACTS 19-28

Paul is speaking with the Ephesians and preparing for his next phase. He makes plans, but they don't always work out as he may expect. We have seen this in the previous attacks, imprisonments, as well as movements of God to free Peter, John, and Paul. There are lessons in these last chapters of Acts. Let's continue.

Acts 19 in Ephesus.

⁸ And he entered the synagogue and continued speaking out boldly for *three months*, reasoning and persuading *them* about the kingdom of God. ⁹ But when some were becoming hardened and disobedient, speaking evil of the Way before the people, he withdrew from them and took away the disciples, reasoning daily in the school of Tyrannus. ¹⁰ This

> took place for _two years_, so that all who lived in Asia heard the word of the Lord, both Jews and Greeks.
>
> ²¹ Now after these things were finished, Paul purposed in the Spirit to go to Jerusalem after he had passed through Macedonia and Achaia, saying, "_After I have been there, I must also see Rome._"

Paul stays in Ephesus for more than two years. He writes to the Corinthians and the expanding Roman Empire. Paul writes a complex intellectual letter, deep with theological teachings. He writes to Rome, the center of the Empire, not because he founded the church or knew much about what was happening, but because he wished to make his own connection with the influential inhabitants of Rome. He may have felt called to bring these literal "movers and shakers" into relationship with the growing church, even as Paul himself remained in the far-reaching communities.

When We Make Plans And God Has Another

As Paul writes Romans, he believes he will visit them soon. But God has other plans. What we see in Acts is Paul's three-to-four-year imprisonment and his protection from Jews out to kill him.

In Acts 20, Paul visits the churches in Greece.

> ² When he had gone through those districts and had given them much exhortation, he came to _Greece_. ³ And _there_ he spent _three months_, and when a plot was formed against him by the Jews as he was about to set sail for Syria, he decided to return through Macedonia.

⁶ We sailed from Philippi after the days of Unleavened Bread, and came to them at Troas within *five days*; and there we stayed *seven days*.

¹⁶ For Paul had decided to sail *past Ephesus* so that he would not have to spend time in Asia; for he was hurrying to be in Jerusalem, if possible, on the *day of Pentecost*.

Luke is keeping a travel journal as Paul heads back to Jerusalem, not that the number of days in each place has significance, other than to show that Luke is now with Paul. Paul decides to pass on a stop in Ephesus. Luke records that one of Paul's motivations is to get to Jerusalem by the day of Pentecost. It is apparent that this Pentecost is significant to Paul.

For me, the Ascension and Pentecost are becoming my significant moments of remembrance. Ascension reminds me that "Jesus is gone," and Pentecost reminds me that we have a "living God" today. Both Ascension and Pentecost give me pause to reflect on the fact that there is a "Holy Spirit" and that I should consider these events and their influence on my life.

²² And now, behold, bound by *the Spirit*, I am on my way to Jerusalem, not knowing what will happen to me there, ²³ except that *the Holy Spirit* solemnly testifies to me in every city, saying that bonds and afflictions await me. ²⁴ But I do not consider my life of any account as dear to myself, so that I may finish my course and the ministry which I received from the Lord Jesus, *to testify solemnly of the gospel of the grace of God*.

The later part of this text is frequently referenced and yet, it is Paul being guided by the Holy Spirit that reminds us that it should not be enough to simply teach accurately. Paul is moved by what the Holy Spirit is guiding him to do. The decisions he makes are not purely rational, but a deferral to the power of God, which guides Paul in his next steps.

> [29] I know that after my departure savage wolves will come in among you, not sparing the flock; [30] and from among your own selves men will arise, speaking perverse things, <u>to draw away the disciples after them</u>.

Sometimes What Is Not Written Is Important

Paul laments what may happen when he's gone. He doesn't take action to instruct them to set up elders and overseers to protect the flock. That's missing here, yet four or five years later Paul does write to Timothy about putting in place overseers and elders to "protect the flock." When you read over and over all the letters, it is worth considering what is not written as much as it is to consider what's there. Here is a case of Paul omitting any discussion of his future concern. To be more specific, this concern is about false teachers who attempt to draw a following.

Therefore, if you hear claims that a person is a false teacher and they are not actively attempting to draw people away from their congregation, it may be that the issue does not reach the level that Paul is concerned about here.

Paul, Luke, and others continue the journey.

⁸ On the next day we left and came to Caesarea, and entering the house of _Philip_ the evangelist, who was _one of the seven_, we stayed with him. ⁹ Now this man had _four virgin daughters_ who were _prophetesses_.

Philip is back, and he has daughters. So much for celibate priests, or perhaps that comes later. Also, a shout-out to all the Beth Moore fans. Let her teach; she might be a prophetess!

¹⁰ As _we_ were staying there for some days, _a prophet_ named _Agabus_ came down from Judea. ¹¹ And coming to us, he took Paul's belt and bound his own feet and hands, and said, "_This is what the Holy Spirit says: 'In this way the Jews at Jerusalem will bind the man who owns this belt and deliver him into the hands of the Gentiles._'" ¹² When _we_ had heard this, _we_ as well as the local residents _began_ begging him not to go up to Jerusalem. ¹³ _Then Paul_ answered, "What are you doing, _weeping_ and _breaking my heart_? For _I am ready_ not only to be bound, but even _to die at Jerusalem_ for the name of the Lord Jesus." ¹⁴ And since he would not be persuaded, we fell silent, remarking, "_The will of the Lord be done!_"

This is an opportunity to ask a few questions. The Holy Spirit informs Agabus that Paul will be bound, and one might believe that Paul would at this point avoid continuing, yet we see Paul's boldness. His team is concerned for him. This includes Luke, who inserts himself into the narrative by using the pronoun "we." Is the Holy Spirit giving Agabus information to change Paul's mind? Or is it simply that God wanted us to know that Paul was heading into difficult circumstances?

He continues and the opposition mounts.

> [27] When the seven days were almost over, the Jews from Asia, upon seeing him in the temple, <u>began to stir up all the crowd</u> and laid hands on him, [28] crying out, "Men of Israel, come to our aid! This is the man who preaches to all men everywhere *against our people* and *the Law* and this place; and besides he has *even brought Greeks into the temple* and has defiled this holy place." [29] For they had previously seen Trophimus the Ephesian in the city with him, and they supposed that Paul had brought him into the temple. [30] Then *all the city was provoked*, and the people rushed together, and taking hold of Paul they *dragged him out of the temple*, and immediately the doors were shut. [31] While they were *seeking to kill him*, a report came up to the commander of the *Roman* cohort that all Jerusalem was in confusion.

Potential Confusion

The pressure of which Agabus is coming to fruition. Nevertheless, it appears that Paul ignored the warning. Yet, perhaps Agabus was called by the Spirit to warn Paul, and Paul was called by the Spirit not to heed his advice. As we move into Acts 22, Paul makes his concluding statements to the people in Jerusalem.

> [20] And when the blood of Your witness Stephen was being shed, I also was standing by approving, and watching out for the coats of those who were slaying him. [21] And He said to me, "*Go! For I will send you far away to the Gentiles.*"
>
> [22] They listened to him <u>up to this statement</u>, and *then* they raised their voices and said, "<u>Away with such a fellow from the earth, for he should not be allowed to live!</u>"

The details of this conflict continue in Acts 23. Paul is brought before the council, and we should give him appreciation for his cleverness under pressure.

> ⁶ But perceiving that one group were _Sadducees_ and the other _Pharisees_, Paul _began_ crying out in the Council, "Brethren, I am a Pharisee, a son of Pharisees; I am on trial for the hope and _Resurrection of the dead!_" ⁷ As he said this, there occurred a _dissension between_ the Pharisees and Sadducees, and the assembly was divided.

This tactic of dividing the Sadducees and Pharisees over the issue of Resurrection wasn't completely effective in obtaining Paul's release. However shrewd Paul may have been, he is not out of his predicament.

> ¹¹ But on the night _immediately_ following, _the Lord_ stood at his side and said, "_Take courage; for as you have solemnly witnessed to My cause at Jerusalem, so you must witness at Rome also._"

Paul is not clear, yet this confirmation from the Lord must have raised his confidence. There also seems to be something special about Rome, as God indicates that no matter what is happening in this moment, Paul will eventually travel to Rome. And we notice it must not be urgent, because this imprisonment is going to go on for three to four years, starting with a conspiracy, which God intervenes to disrupt.

> ¹⁶ _But_ the son of _Paul's sister_ heard of their ambush, and he came and entered the barracks and _told Paul_.

Here's a miraculous intervention. When I read about God intervening, I often "preach" to myself. Where in my life do I pray for God's presence? Could it be that it only takes someone with whom we have passing familiarity to extend the hand of grace? Here, God uses Paul's nephew to bring key information to him. From there, a better decision is made.

> [20] And he said, "The Jews have agreed to ask you to bring Paul down tomorrow to the Council, *as though* they were going to inquire somewhat more thoroughly about him. [21] So do not listen to them, for *more than 40* of them are *lying in wait* for him who have bound themselves under a curse not to eat or drink *until they slay him*; and now they are ready and waiting for the promise from you."

More Shade For Paul

These Jewish people really hated Paul. This is intense persecution and we see God intervening to protect him. We know their attempts to kill Paul were not successful. Paul is not making decisions here. His ability to act is limited. And yet he lives on as others make decisions that will impact his future.

> [31] So the soldiers, in accordance with their orders, took Paul and brought him by night to Antipatris. [32] But the next day, leaving the horsemen to go on with him, they returned to the barracks. [33] When these had come to Caesarea and delivered the letter to the governor, they also presented Paul to him.

The unfolding of this drama is getting considerable attention from Luke. It certainly is interesting, and the longer it goes I wonder why there's not an early release. Is not Paul critical to achieving the Great Commission? Is not God the one that has been acting this whole time to remove his leaders from peril, prison, persecution? The details continue in Acts 24.

> After five days the high priest Ananias came down with some elders, with *an attorney named Tertullus*, and they brought charges to the governor against Paul. ² After *Paul* had been summoned, *Tertullus* began to accuse him, saying *to the governor*,

> "Since we have *through you* attained *much peace,* and since by your providence *reforms are being carried out* for this nation, ³ we acknowledge *this* in every way and everywhere, *most excellent Felix,* with *all thankfulness.* ⁴ But, that I may not weary you any further, I beg you to grant us, *by your kindness, a brief hearing*."

We have a clever lawyer working with his words to get what he wants in this trial. On the one hand, it is very devious. The lawyer may not really wish to have justice, but simply set up a transport from Caesaria to Jerusalem to kill Paul on the way.

> ⁵ For we have found this man *a real pest* and a fellow who *stirs up dissension* among *all the Jews* throughout *the world,* and *a ringleader* of the sect of the Nazarenes. ⁶ And he even tried to *desecrate the temple*; and then we arrested him.

> ⁹ *The Jews* also joined in the attack, asserting that these things were so.

The prosecution does not like Paul. Nevertheless, Paul makes a fine defense and lives another day.

The Sixth Sola

> ²⁷ But after *two years* had passed, Felix was succeeded by Porcius Festus, and wishing to do the Jews a favor, Felix left Paul imprisoned.

This imprisonment is not like the previous ones when he is let out within 24 hours. Two years! What must Paul be thinking? Could he be frustrated and asking why this is taking so long? Here with Felix and now a new governor Festus, we continue in Acts 25:

> ⁷ After Paul arrived, the Jews who had come down from Jerusalem stood around him, bringing *many and serious charges against him* which they could not prove, ⁸ while Paul said in his own defense, "I have committed no offense either against the Law of the Jews or against the temple or against Caesar." ⁹ But Festus, *wishing to do the Jews a favor*, answered Paul and said, "Are you willing to go up to Jerusalem and stand trial before me on these *charges*?" ¹⁰ But Paul said, "*I am standing before Caesar's tribunal, where I ought to be tried. I have done no wrong to the Jews, as you also very well know*.

The level of intensity in the Jewish people's hatred for Paul is strong. They have not forgotten Paul in prison, but two years later they are still after him. And Paul maintains his composure and purposes that there is no need to go back to Jerusalem. He was standing his ground. Paul remains with Festus, and King Agrippa arrives as we move into the next chapter.

> ²² So, having obtained *help from God*, I stand to this day testifying both to small and great, stating nothing but what the Prophets and Moses said was going to take

place; ²³ that the Christ was to suffer, *and* that by reason of <u>His Resurrection</u> from the dead He would be <u>the first to proclaim light</u> both to <u>the Jewish people</u> and to <u>the Gentiles</u>.

The theme of the book of Acts is that this message is for both Jews and Gentiles.

²⁴ While *Paul* was saying this in his defense, Festus *said in a loud voice, "<u>Paul, you are out of your mind! Your great learning is driving you mad</u>." ²⁵ But Paul *said, "I am not out of my mind, most excellent Festus, but I utter <u>words of sober truth</u>. ²⁶ For the king knows about these matters, and I speak to him also with confidence, since I am persuaded that none of these things escape his notice; for this has not been done in a corner. ²⁷ King Agrippa, do you believe the Prophets? I know that you do." ²⁸ Agrippa *replied* to Paul, "<u>In a short time you will persuade me to become a Christian</u>." ²⁹ And Paul *said*, "I would wish to God, that whether in a short or long time, not only you, but also <u>all who hear me this day, might become such as I am, except for these chains</u>."

What Is All The Fuss About?

Note, after these years, Agrippa is familiar with the term Christian. Paul is proclaiming the message and Agrippa is not moved. The other theme is that God affects conversion, not just the right words. The words were sufficient. We see that if it were time for Agrippa to respond in another manner, he would.

³⁰ The king stood up and the governor and Bernice, and those who were sitting with them, ³¹ and when they had gone aside, they *began* talking to one another, saying, "<u>This man</u>

is not doing anything worthy of death or imprisonment."³² And Agrippa said to Festus, "This man might have been *set free* if he had not appealed to Caesar."

The conclusion is that Paul did nothing worthy of death after nearly four years.

We are getting close to the end of this journey Luke has taken us on in the book of Acts. Chapter 27 continues with travel to Rome. The ship sets sail and the weather becomes an issue.

⁹ When considerable time had passed and the voyage was *now dangerous*, since even the fast was already over, Paul *began* to admonish them, ¹⁰ and said to them, "*Men, I perceive that the voyage will certainly be with damage and great loss, not only of the cargo and the ship, but also of our lives.*" ¹¹ But *the centurion* was *more persuaded* by *the pilot* and *the captain* of the ship than by what was being said by Paul.

Paul made his attempt to influence the decision whether to stay or go and he didn't win them all.

²⁰ Since neither sun nor stars appeared for many days, and no small storm was assailing *us*, from then on *all hope of our being saved was gradually abandoned*.

²¹ When they had gone a long time without food, then Paul stood up in their midst and said, "*Men, you ought to have followed my advice and not to have set sail from Crete and incurred this damage and loss.* ²² *Yet* now I urge you to keep up your courage, for there will be no loss of life among you, but *only* of the ship.²³ For *this very night an angel* of *the God to*

> *whom I belong* and whom I serve stood before me, ²⁴ saying, '*Do not be afraid, Paul; you must stand before Caesar; and behold, God has granted you all those who are sailing with you.*' ²⁵ Therefore, keep up your courage, men, for I believe God that it will turn out exactly as I have been told. ²⁶ But we must run aground on a certain island."

In the events leading to Paul's arrival in Rome, God is intervening once again.

> ³⁰ But as the sailors were trying to escape from the ship and had let down the *ship's* boat into the sea, on the pretense of intending to lay out anchors from the bow, ³¹ Paul said to the centurion and to the soldiers, "*Unless* these men remain in the ship, you yourselves cannot be saved." ³² Then the soldiers cut away the ropes of the *ship's* boat and let it fall away.

They listened to Paul this time. Well done, but they're not in the clear yet.

> ⁴² The soldiers' plan was *to kill the prisoners*, so that none *of them* would swim away and escape; ⁴³ but the centurion, wanting to bring Paul safely through, kept them from their intention, and commanded that those who could swim should jump overboard first and get to land, ⁴⁴ and the rest *should follow*, some on planks, and others on various things from the ship. *And so it happened that they all were brought safely to land*.

We then move into the final chapter, Acts 28. The ending of the beginning.

The Sixth Sola

²³ When they had set a day for Paul, they came to him at his lodging in large numbers; and he was explaining to them by solemnly testifying about the kingdom of God and *trying to persuade them concerning Jesus*, from both the Law of Moses and from the Prophets, from morning until evening. **²⁴** *Some were being persuaded by the things spoken*, but others would not believe. **²⁵** And when they did not agree with one another, *they began leaving* after Paul had spoken *one parting word*,

"The Holy Spirit rightly spoke through Isaiah the prophet to your fathers, **²⁶** saying,

'Go to this people and say, "You will keep on hearing, but will not understand;

And you will keep on seeing, but will not perceive;

²⁷ For the heart of this people has become dull, And with their ears they scarcely hear, And they have closed their eyes;

Otherwise they might see with their eyes, And hear with their ears, And understand with their heart and return, And I would heal them.'"

²⁸ Therefore let it be known to you that *this salvation of God has been sent to the Gentiles*; they will also listen." **²⁹** When he had spoken these words, *the Jews departed*, having a great dispute among themselves.

³⁰ And *he stayed two full years in his own rented quarters* and was welcoming all who came to him, **³¹** preaching the kingdom of God and teaching concerning the Lord Jesus Christ with all openness, unhindered.

And that's the end, the theme of how Gentiles and Jews are incorporated together, along with the active working of God and the Holy Spirit. For me, this sets the overview for the letters Paul wrote during his missionary journeys. We see many of the concerns he had as well as his attitude toward the people he was meeting. The books and letters we have from Paul may be divided between those written early, in the midst of his travels, and later after his imprisonments, including his final imprisonment in Rome.

The Sola Spiritu Ambulatio as the Sixth Sola is a framework for living and fulfilling our calling. It is foundational to Paul's writings. The core passage for the Spiritu Ambulatio comes from Paul's letter to the Galatians. I set out to consider how Paul brings this forth from the discussion on circumcision in the book of Acts because if we are not looking at historical context and larger passages of Scripture, we may quite often miss the essential message that God has provided for us.

CHAPTER 8

SOLA SPIRITU AMBULATIO

Welcome to the core message: Sola Spiritu Ambulatio.

Luke has given us an overview of what took place from the Ascension to Paul's arrival in Rome, which is a period of 20 to 30 years. It began with Christ's departure, the coming Holy Spirit, and the actions of Peter, John, and Philip. Eventually we reach Saul, who becomes Paul with Barnabas. These people were on a journey.

After reading the book of Acts, we enter into the heart of Paul's messages. I come from a traditional position. While many books have been written about their authorship, I am seeking what all these words and letters were communicating and why they are important.

As we saw earlier, there is a debate in Galatia about the need for Gentiles to be circumcised. We know from reading

Acts that this topic was debated and resolved, and it was agreed that circumcision was not going to be required for Gentiles. In Galatians, word has come back to Paul that others are proclaiming that Gentiles still must be circumcised. This is what Paul takes on in this letter.

Galatians 1

1 Paul, an apostle (*not sent from men* nor through the agency of man, *but through Jesus Christ and God the Father*, who raised Him from the dead), **²** and all the brethren who are with me,

To *the churches of Galatia*:

³ *Grace* to you and *peace* from God our Father and the Lord Jesus Christ, **⁴** who gave Himself for our sins so that He might *rescue us* from this *present evil age*, according to the will of our God and Father, **⁵** to whom *be* the glory forevermore. Amen.

Paul has moved from being Saul to Paul. He reminds readers that he is not sent from men, but through Jesus Christ. Readers are familiar with Paul's history of initially attacking the faith, now laboring for it.

He addresses the churches in the region of Galatia, and they have specific situations which Paul will discuss. He begins with well-wishes for Grace and Peace. And he references the gospel of Jesus, rescuing readers from their circumstances and the implied hope it carries.

⁶ I am *amazed* that you are so quickly *deserting Him* who *called you* by *the grace of Christ*, for *a different gospel*; **⁷** which is *really not another*; only there are some who are disturbing you and want to *distort the gospel* of Christ. ⁸ But even if we, or an angel from heaven, should *preach to you a gospel contrary* to what we have preached to you, he is to be accursed! ⁹ As we have said before, so I say again now, if any man is *preaching to you a gospel contrary* to what you *received*, he is to be accursed!

There's something that is causing Paul to conclude that the Galatians are "deserting" the gospel of Jesus. The one positive is that they did "receive" the original gospel brought by Paul, so perhaps they are just confused and need Paul to provide clarification on the faith.

¹⁰ For am I now seeking *the favor of men*, or of *God?* Or am I striving to please men? If I were still trying to please men, I would *not be a bond-servant of Christ*.

¹¹ For I would have you know, brethren, that *the gospel* which was preached by me is not according to man. ¹² For I neither received it from man, nor was I taught it, but *I received it* through a *revelation of Jesus Christ*.

Paul is establishing his credibility. He's serving Christ and makes the claim that what he expressed is not according to man, and that he received it from a revelation of Jesus Christ.

¹³ For you have heard of my *former manner of life in Judaism*, how I used to *persecute the church of God* beyond measure and *tried to destroy it*; ¹⁴ and I was advancing in Judaism beyond many of my contemporaries among my countrymen, being *more extremely zealous* for my ancestral traditions. ¹⁵ *But when*

> _God_, who had set me apart _even_ from my mother's womb and called me through His grace, was pleased ¹⁶ to _reveal His Son in me_ so that I might _preach Him among the Gentiles_, I _did not_ immediately _consult with flesh and blood_,¹⁷ nor did I go up to Jerusalem to those who were apostles before me; but I went away to Arabia, and returned once more to Damascus.

That Wily Paul

Paul continues with his credentials, building a case about why they should listen to him. He backs up his claim of not being sent by men by explaining that he did not consult with men, rather he went on to consider the impact of his life. I don't believe Paul would deny that he was led by the Holy Spirit. He's acknowledging all his beliefs and teachings are from God.

> ¹⁸ Then three years later I went up to Jerusalem to become _acquainted with Cephas_, and stayed with him fifteen days. ¹⁹ But I did not see any other of the apostles except James, the Lord's brother. ²⁰ (Now in what I am writing to you, I assure you before God that _I am not lying_.) ²¹ Then I went into the regions of Syria and Cilicia. ²² I was _still_ unknown by sight to the churches of Judea which were in Christ; ²³ but only, they kept hearing, "_He who once persecuted us is now preaching the faith which he once tried to destroy_." ²⁴ And they were glorifying God because of me.

Paul concludes with his eventual contact with the "originals" and his comment about "not lying." He's not adding to his credentials by saying, "I am now writing to you the inerrant, God-inspired word." And yet Paul is not writing in a trance, dictating words from God himself. This is that complexity of seeing the human element in writing and yet at the same time, the inspired Word of God.

Galatians 2 begins to address the specifics of the issue at hand.

2 Then after an interval of fourteen years I went up again to Jerusalem with Barnabas, taking Titus along also. ² It was because of *a revelation* that I went up; and I submitted to them *the gospel* which I preach among the Gentiles, but *I did so* in private to those who were of reputation, for fear that I might be running, or had run, in vain. ³ But not even Titus, who was with me, *though he was a Greek, was compelled to be circumcised*. ⁴ But *it was* because of the *false brethren secretly brought in*, who had *sneaked in to spy out our liberty* which we have in Christ Jesus, in order to *bring us into bondage*. ⁵ But we did not yield in subjection to them *for even an hour*, so that *the truth of the gospel* would remain with you. ⁶ But from those who were of *high reputation* (what they were makes no difference to me; God shows no partiality)—well, those who were of reputation *contributed nothing to me*. ⁷ But on the contrary, seeing that I had been entrusted with the gospel to *the uncircumcised*, just as *Peter had been to the circumcised* ⁸ (for *He* who effectually *worked* for *Peter* in *his* apostleship *to the circumcised* effectually *worked* for *me* also *to the Gentiles*), ⁹ and recognizing the grace that had been given to me, James and Cephas and John, who were reputed to be pillars, gave to me and Barnabas the right hand of fellowship, so that *we might go to the Gentiles* and *they to the circumcised*. ¹⁰ *They* only *asked* us to *remember the poor*—the very thing I also was eager to do.

More Circumcision Or Boundary Markers

Here, it is revealed that the issue Paul is concerned with is whether Gentiles should be circumcised. In John 7:22–24, Jesus briefly mentions circumcision in defense of healing a man on the Sabbath. However, the debate took place as we read the book of Acts. It was settled back then that Gentiles did not need to be circumcised. And Paul refers to Titus as one who was not circumcised and yet a worker and leader.

Paul uses language that certain men wanted to compel Gentiles to be circumcised and put them in bondage. Is the temptation to control believers with added constraints something that occurs more frequently than we might imagine?

> [11] But when Cephas *came to Antioch*, I *opposed him to his face*, because he stood condemned. [12] For prior to the coming of certain men from James, he *used to eat with the Gentiles*; but when they came, he *began to withdraw and hold himself aloof*, fearing *the party of the circumcision*. [13] The rest of the Jews joined him in *hypocrisy*, with the result that *even Barnabas* was carried away by *their hypocrisy*. [14] But when I saw that they were *not straightforward* about the truth of the gospel, I said to Cephas in the presence of all, "*If you, being a Jew, live like the Gentiles and not like the Jews, how is it that you compel the Gentiles to live like Jews?*

Wow, not only is this circumcision deeply felt among the traditional Jewish culture, but Paul is also sensitive to the slight behaviors of Peter such that he "opposes Peter to his face." Do you have some that have added to the gospel in your life? They seemingly communicate that it's not good enough to have faith, that you are not good enough to live out your faith. Perhaps they want to hold a position of authority over you and quote Hebrews 13:7 about obeying your leaders and submitting to them, and yet there's been no instruction. It's just another verse pluck to somehow judge your behavior. At least we have Paul mentioning these people in 2 Corinthians 11 when he refers to "false brethren." Sadly, it can happen. Perhaps some people in your life need to be opposed to their face.

> [15] We *are* Jews by nature and not sinners from among the Gentiles;[16] nevertheless knowing that a man is *not justified by the works of the Law* but through *faith in Christ Jesus*, *even we* have *believed in Christ Jesus*, so that we may be *justified by faith* in Christ and *not by* the works of the Law; since by the works of the Law no flesh will be justified. [17] But if, while seeking to be justified in Christ, we ourselves have also been found sinners, is Christ then a minister of sin? May it never be! [18] For if I rebuild what I have *once* destroyed, I prove myself to be a transgressor. [19] For through the Law *I died to the Law*, so that I might live to God. [20] I have been *crucified with Christ*; and it is no longer I who live, but *Christ lives in me*; and the *life* which I now live in *the flesh I live* by *faith in the Son of God*, who *loved me* and *gave Himself* up for me. [21] I *do not* nullify *the grace* of God, for if *righteousness comes* through the Law, then *Christ died needlessly*.

This section has theological concepts that form the foundation of most Reformed and Protestant churches, especially in terms of justification and the forgiveness of our sins. Paul is referring to the law that says justification is through circumcision, yet they all agreed it was not, and this entire section of Paul's discussion is simply on the "body language" of Peter. Paul is very sensitive to Peter's behavior. He goes on to explain that he died to this law.

This is an oft-quoted passage, and "verse plucking" style is often preached as a standalone message. We need to go on foreign missions to be right with God. It says so in Matthew 28:19, 20. You must "die to yourselves." See, it's right here in Galatians 2:20.

This type of teaching is similar to teaching we have to be circumcised. It's adding to the Law. I am not opposed to foreign missions; if the Holy Spirit calls people to them, then they should go. Some are sent for less than reasons of a call. Here, can we not look at the entire message and see that Paul is "doing the Great Commission"? He doesn't need anyone to exhort or implore him to do it, and as I read all of Paul's writings, I have yet to see him exhort anyone to do what he does. Ironically, when he's instructing Timothy on leading the Ephesian church, he says nothing about sending out others. Paul just does it. No fanfare, no conferences about reaching unreached groups. Yes, I'm like Paul, sensitive to those adding law back into the gospel. It's right here. Peter himself did it. He was opposed.

This chapter ends with the complexity about dying to the Law. While it is not easy to comprehend, the phrase "Christ lives in me" may be the Holy Spirit living in Paul. Throughout Paul's writings and even today, we speak about Christ living in us. Yet is it better to speak of the Holy Spirit? In some ways, they are equivalent.

Who Is The Fool?

Galatians 3

> ³ You _foolish Galatians_, who has bewitched you, before whose eyes _Jesus Christ_ was publicly portrayed _as crucified_? ² This is the only thing I want to find out from you: _did you receive the Spirit by the works of the Law, or by hearing with faith_? ³ Are you _so foolish_? Having _begun by the Spirit,_ are you now _being perfected by the flesh_? ⁴ Did you suffer so many things in vain—if indeed it was in vain? ⁵ So then, does _He_ who provides you with _the Spirit_ and works miracles among you, _do it_ by the _works of the Law_, or by _hearing with faith_?

To call the Galatians foolish is an aggressive statement. And yet, that's a reflection of how strong his feelings are on these attempts to corrupt the simplicity of the gospel. Once again, the question is similar to Acts 19:2. I would say there's a theme of asking about whether one received the Holy Spirit. Here it is in terms of asking under what circumstances one might receive the Holy Spirit, whether by works of the Law or by hearing the gospel and coming to faith. Do we have the Spirit by Law or by faith?

> ⁶ Even so Abraham _believed God_, and it was reckoned to him as righteousness.⁷ Therefore, be sure that it is _those who are of faith_ who are sons of Abraham.⁸ _The Scripture_, foreseeing that _God would justify the Gentiles by faith_, preached the gospel beforehand to Abraham, _saying_, "_All the nations will be blessed in you._" ⁹ So then those who are _of faith_ are blessed with Abraham, _the believer_.

The Sixth Sola

Paul makes the connection between Abraham's belief and God's intention to bring the Gentiles in by the same faith. Blessings to all nations through Abraham, the believer.

> [10] For as many as are of the works of the Law are under a curse; for it is written, "Cursed is everyone who does not abide by all things written in the book of the law, to perform them." [11] Now that _no one_ is _justified by the Law_ before God is evident; for, "The righteous man shall _live by faith_." [12] However, the Law is not of faith; on the contrary, "He who practices them shall live by them." [13] _Christ redeemed us_ from the curse of the Law, having become a curse for us—for it is written, "Cursed is everyone who hangs on a tree"— [14] in order that _in Christ Jesus_ the _blessing of Abraham_ might come to _the Gentiles_, so that we would receive _the promise_ of _the Spirit_ through _faith._

The blessings to Abraham now come to the Gentiles through faith. That was the promise of the Spirit.

> [15] Brethren, I speak in terms of human relations: even though it is _only_ a man's covenant, yet when it has been ratified, no one sets it aside or adds conditions to it. [16] Now _the promises_ were spoken to Abraham and to his seed. He does not say, "And to seeds," as _referring_ to many, but _rather_ to one, "_And to your seed_," that is, _Christ._ [17] What I am saying is this: the Law, which came _four hundred and thirty years later_, does not invalidate a covenant previously ratified by God, so as to _nullify the promise_. [18] For if _the inheritance_ is based on law, it is no longer based on a promise; but God has granted it to Abraham by _means of a promise_.

Are We Speaking To Jews Or Gentiles

Paul further connects the promises to Abraham and how that through Christ, these promises exist from 430 years earlier than the Law. Paul is connecting Israel's history to the Gentiles, now that Jesus Christ has fulfilled his mission.

> [19] Why the Law then? It was added because of transgressions, having been ordained through angels by the agency of a mediator, until the seed would come to whom the promise had been made. [20] Now a mediator is not for one *party only*; whereas God is *only* one. [21] Is the Law then contrary to the promises of God? May it never be! *For if a law had been given which was able to impart life, then righteousness would indeed have been based on law.* [22] But *the Scripture* has shut up everyone under sin, so that *the promise by faith* in Jesus Christ might be *given to those who believe.*

This is more on the Law, Scripture, and promises through faith as a gift to those who believe. Notice that life could never be imparted through the Law. This life is given through the promised Holy Spirit. I suspect Martin Luther wrote much about these passages.

There are many books documenting and explaining this distinction between works and grace. In particular, Luther argues with Erasmus, leading to Luther's writings on the "Bondage of the Will." This was his argument for only by faith. Paul writes plainly. And remember this is the 16th century. Not many people read, and the religious structure is established. There are not many people inside the organization questioning their teachings. Recall, the priests were powerful as they read for their people and verbally dispensed "knowledge."

> ²³ But before faith came, <u>we </u>were kept in custody under the Law, being shut up to the faith which was later to be revealed. ²⁴ Therefore the Law has become our tutor *to lead us* to Christ, so that we may be <u>*justified by faith*</u>. ²⁵ But now that <u>*faith*</u> has come, we are no longer under a tutor. ²⁶ For you are <u>*all sons of God*</u> through <u>*faith*</u> in Christ Jesus. ²⁷ For all of you who were <u>*baptized into Christ*</u> have clothed yourselves with Christ. ²⁸ There is <u>*neither Jew nor Greek*</u>, there is neither <u>*slave nor free man*</u>, there is neither <u>*male nor female*</u>; for you are <u>*all one in Christ Jesus*</u>.²⁹ And <u>*if you belong to Christ*</u>, then you are <u>*Abraham's descendants*</u>, <u>*heirs according to promise*</u>.

Paul ends here with additional clarification for Jews who have been adherents to the Law. For Gentiles, these words explain how the faith has come to them as well. We are all one in Christ, whether Jew or Greek, slave or free, male or female. We are heirs according to the promise to Abraham's descendants, as long as we belong to Christ. Paul is continuing to build his case for letting the instructions from the Law, specifically the circumcision, be overruled by faith.

Sweet Inheritance

Galatians 4

> 4 Now I say, as long as <u>*the heir*</u> is a child, he does not differ at all from a slave although he is owner of everything, ² but he is <u>*under guardians and managers*</u> until the date set by the father. ³ So also we, while we were children, were <u>*held in bondage*</u> under <u>*the elemental things*</u> of the world. ⁴ But when the fullness of the time came, God sent forth His Son, born of a woman, born under the Law, ⁵ so that He might <u>*redeem*</u> those

who were under the Law, that we might *receive the adoption as sons*. ⁶ Because you are sons, *God has sent forth the Spirit of His Son* into *our hearts*, crying, "Abba! Father!" ⁷ Therefore you are *no longer a slave*, but a son; and if a son, then an *heir through God*.

Paul adds language concerning inheritance and heirs. He speaks of bondage to the world, and that Jesus came to redeem those under the law as adopted sons. Then the ownership of the Spirit is sent into our hearts. This is not a measurable act, though perhaps it does bring experiential shifts. This subject will return in Galatians 5. Paul is building his argument against circumcision, but also an external relationship with God based on our actions, and not on the actions of God, which are the actions of the Holy Spirit.

⁸ However *at that time*, when you *did not know God*, you were slaves to those which by nature are no gods. ⁹ But now that you have come to know God, or rather to *be known by God*, how is it that you *turn back again* to the *weak and worthless elemental things*, to which you desire to be enslaved all over again?¹⁰ *You observe days and months and seasons and years*. ¹¹ I fear for you, that perhaps I have labored over you in vain.

Paul recalls his visit with them and how he brought the gospel message and established the faith not based on works or outward adherence to traditions or law. This is the argument against circumcision. Today, we do not continue this argument specifically over circumcision, but perhaps it shows up in other ways.

Is it possible that incessant calls for fulfilling the Great Commission are the new circumcision? Paul's doing the Great Commission; he doesn't make calls for furtherance of a mission as it is expressed today.

> [12] I beg of you, brethren, _become as I am_, for I also _have become_ as you _are_. You have done me no wrong; [13] but you know that it was because of a bodily illness that I preached the gospel to you the first time; [14] and that which was a trial to you in my bodily condition you did not despise or loathe, but _you received me as an angel of God_, as _Christ Jesus Himself_. [15] _Where then is that sense of blessing you had?_ For I bear you witness that, if possible, you would have plucked out your eyes and given them to me. [16] _So have I become your enemy by telling you the truth?_ [17] _They eagerly seek you_, not commendably, but they wish _to shut you out so that you will seek them_. [18] But it is good always to be eagerly sought in a commendable manner, and not only when I am present with you. [19] My children, with whom _I am again in labor until Christ is formed in you_— [20] but I could wish _to be present with you now_ and to _change my tone_, for I am _perplexed about you_.

Paul brings his personal experience as he reminds them of the circumstances of his coming—an illness in spite of which he persevered. He recalls how the Galatians received him with great eagerness and enthusiasm, as if he were Jesus Christ himself. That's a bold statement, and the flow of the text certainly does not indicate that Paul was boasting.

Are You Sure You Do Not Want Law?

He then makes comments on this other faction attempting to influence the Galatians to comply with the Law and circumcision.

The statement "to shut you out so that you will seek them" is an indication what false teaching is all about. Here, Paul ends with emotional imagery as if he were the mother of these people, in labor pains for them.

> ²¹ Tell me, you who *want to be under law*, do you *not listen to the law*? ²² For it is written that Abraham had *two sons*, one by the *bondwoman* and one by the *free woman*. ²³ But the son by the bondwoman was born according *to the flesh*, and the son by the free woman *through the promise*. ²⁴ This is allegorically speaking, for these *women* are *two covenants*: one *proceeding from Mount Sinai* bearing children who are to be slaves; she is Hagar. ²⁵ Now this Hagar is Mount Sinai in Arabia and corresponds to the present Jerusalem, for *she is in slavery with her children*. ²⁶ But the Jerusalem above *is free*; she is our mother. ²⁷ For it is written,
>
> "Rejoice, barren woman who does not bear; Break forth and shout, you who are not in labor; For more numerous are the *children of the desolate* Than of the one who has a husband."
>
> ²⁸ And you brethren, like Isaac, are *children of promise*. ²⁹ But as at that time he who was born according to *the flesh persecuted him* who was *born according to the Spirit*, so *it is now also*. ³⁰ But what does the Scripture say?
>
> "Cast out the bondwoman and her son, For the son of the bondwoman shall not be an heir with the son of the free woman."
>
> ³¹ So then, brethren, we are *not children* of a *bondwoman, but* of the free woman.

The conclusion here is to consider ourselves the children of the free woman. This is the covenant of promise. We can look back and see this from Jewish history, their Scriptures, which now are our Scriptures. We are essentially one people, though the division between Jew and Gentile is something that Paul was working out with Peter and others as the Holy Spirit led. Certainly, we see Paul speaking to and on behalf of the Gentiles.

Paul appreciates this, as does Peter. That being said, they are not in complete agreement on how to proceed. Those growing up with strict adherence to a written Law are not all moving over to this new covenant based on this mystery of Jesus. The Jews are fine if they are the people Jesus came to reconcile, but we see that they are not as keen to understand that it is for the Gentiles as well. Additionally, the idea that there is nothing to add to what Christ has accomplished is difficult for those with a history of performing acts and ceremonies to fulfill their covenant relationship.

These first four chapters lead up to the promise of freedom through the Holy Spirit. That is the power Paul sees at work in his preaching. Paul is writing this letter not from the position of a scholar but as one bringing the message of the Spirit to the many cities that are within his reach.

This letter is meant to settle the question of circumcision once and for all. The idea that Gentiles would be circumcised makes sense to Jews, and yet the Gentiles are listening for Paul and others to explain what is important. Paul has built the case that the gospel is the new covenant. Here, Paul is connecting the Law versus the Spirit with the traditions of Hagar and Sarah. This next chapter brings us to the Sola Spiritu Ambulatio.

Freedom

Galatians 5

> ⁵ It was for *freedom* that *Christ* set us *free*; therefore keep standing firm and *do not* be *subject* again to a *yoke of slavery*.

Paul continues with freedom; this new covenant is about freedom and he describes the previous Jewish relationship with God as similar to slavery to Law.

> ² Behold I, *Paul*, say to you that *if you receive circumcision*, Christ will be of *no benefit to you*. ³ And I testify again to every man who receives circumcision, that he is under obligation to *keep the whole Law*. ⁴ You have been *severed from Christ*, you who are seeking to be *justified by law*; you have *fallen from grace*. ⁵ For we through *the Spirit*, *by faith*, are waiting for *the hope* of righteousness. ⁶ For in Christ Jesus *neither circumcision nor uncircumcision* means anything, but *faith working* through *love*.

My response to these words is, wow. Paul goes right at the circumcision by first declaring that it is of no benefit. He even puts an added burden on anyone who chooses to proceed with it, that they are bound to some extent to keep the whole law. According to this view, continuing with the practices of the old covenant is an attempt to be justified without the grace that God offers us.

Paul connects faith, hope, and love through the Spirit. With this new covenant, we have hope that our righteousness comes through faith, and that as a result, our faith will result in how people love.

The Sixth Sola

Today, do we experience any kind of teaching that may be considered a legalistic constraint? There may be religious organizations that give the impression that to be really good, special, and pleasing to the Lord, extra effort is due from us. This additional boundary marker is a return to legalistic thinking. Paul is expressing the amazing freedom we have to be in this new covenant of grace.

> ⁷ You were running well; *who* hindered you from *obeying the truth*? ⁸ This persuasion *did* not *come* from *Him who calls you*. ⁹ A little leaven leavens the whole lump *of dough*. ¹⁰ I have confidence in you in the Lord that you will *adopt no other view*; but the one who is disturbing you will bear his judgment, *whoever he is*. ¹¹ But I, brethren, if I still preach circumcision, why am I still persecuted? Then the stumbling block of the cross has been abolished. ¹² I wish that those who are troubling you would even *mutilate themselves*.

Someone is getting in the way of the essential gospel that Paul preaches. Paul is convinced that faith, hope, and love are the directions that God has prepared for us, not a legalistic system of hierarchy and approval by other men. This is not the teaching of "Him who calls you." This is the new covenant; this is the Holy Spirit, Jesus, God the Father. Paul is upset. He wishes those who are teaching otherwise would hurt themselves.

> ¹³ For you were *called to freedom*, brethren; only *do* not *turn* your freedom into an *opportunity for the flesh*, but *through love serve* one another. ¹⁴ For the whole Law is fulfilled in one word, in the *statement*, "*You shall love your neighbor as yourself*." ¹⁵ But if you bite and devour one another, take care that you are *not consumed by one another*.

Flesh vs. Spirit

Paul is returning to "flesh" as an offset to the "Spirit." There is certainly an element of the flesh that wishes to be satisfied, yet the call is also to serve one another in love. This leads to a relationship or service. Then Paul comments about this love for our neighbor. I would think this shift would expose that circumcision is simply a symbolic performance. How would it benefit anyone? Here, Paul is shifting to how we relate to one another.

> [16] But I say, _walk by the Spirit_, and you will _not carry out the desire of the flesh_. [17] For _the flesh_ sets its desire against _the Spirit_, and _the Spirit_ against _the flesh_; for these are in opposition to one another, so that you may not do the things that you please. [18] _But if_ you are _led by the Spirit_, you are _not_ under _the Law_. [19] Now _the deeds_ of _the flesh_ are evident, which are: immorality, impurity, sensuality, [20] idolatry, sorcery, enmities, strife, jealousy, outbursts of anger, disputes, dissensions, factions, [21] envying, drunkenness, carousing, and things like these, of which I forewarn you, just as I have forewarned you, that those who _practice such things_ will _not inherit_ the kingdom of God. [22] _But_ the fruit of _the Spirit_ is _love_, _joy_, _peace_, _patience_, _kindness_, _goodness_, _faithfulness_, [23] _gentleness_, _self-control_; against such things there is _no law_. [24] Now those who _belong to Christ Jesus_ have _crucified the flesh_ with its passions and desires.

And this is it! This is the Sola Spiritu Ambulatio. It's right here. Paul is saying if you want to do something, if you want to live in a righteous relationship with God, then just walk in the Spirit. That's Paul's proposal to us. Are we walking in the Spirit? What does that look like?

Paul asks us whether we are going to walk in the Spirit or walk in the flesh. He's writing to those that have responded to the gospel message. They've even received the Holy Spirit, yet the pull to return to a legalistic, ceremonial, practice of pleasing God is what is causing trouble.

This is opposed to simply having faith. What are we going to choose? Flesh or Spirit?

He says that we can be led by the Spirit and therefore walk in the Spirit. Otherwise, we will likely fall into the deeds of the flesh. Reading the list of negative behaviors may cause one to feel fear, shame, or guilt. We may struggle with some issues of the flesh, yet Paul does add that it is the practice of these deeds that puts us in a tough spot.

When writing of the alternative, Paul does not use imperative language to say that you need to love, have joy, and be patient to walk in the Spirit. He sets these qualities out as behaviors exemplified by the one walking in the Spirit. In other words, these are the fruit of the Spirit.

Most of these nine characteristics are demonstrated in our relationships. So I ask myself, "How are my closest relationships?" For example, when I'm impatient, I ask those closest to me to let me know because I aspire to grow in accepting their feedback. As I've explored this principle in my own life, I have come to realize that God is not expecting perfection. In fact, this is the Great Relationship full of grace.

Not All Or Nothing

If I improve and show more love, more joy, more patience, it is a step in the right direction. Instead of an all-or-nothing framework, I've come to see walking in the Spirit as a growth or sanctification process. At times, that has been a mental challenge for me. I often think about what I can do to be "good" when really, the shift in mindset is about letting myself get started.

This is essentially what I would like from my own behaviors and for others as well. We are human and we often punish ourselves when we compare ourselves with one another. Therefore, a framework of walking in the Spirit would allow opportunities for all of us, with our variety of experiences, to embrace growth one step at a time.

"[25] If we _live by the Spirit_, let us also _walk by the Spirit_. [26] _Let us not become boastful, challenging_ one another, _envying_ one another."

We are reading these words because of our faith in the Spirit. If we have this start by the Spirit, then we are to walk by the Spirit. Paul is giving us this imperative, and really this is the Sixth Sola. Paul didn't name it and yet the principle is here.

Notice he goes on to discourage boasting, challenging, and envying one another. This appears to be his concern about our comparing ourselves to one another.

The fruit of the Spirit is not reducible to yes or no evaluations. I have come to see them as opportunities to get better. And that is how I now understand the sanctification process. Although this book is about transforming ourselves, if we have a community that recognizes our gifts and our shortcomings, we may choose to support one another and start from a place of grace, love, and acceptance.

Paul has one more chapter in Galatians. Let's see how he finishes.

Paul: The Closer

Galatians 6

> [6] Brethren, even if anyone is caught in any trespass, you who are _spiritual_, restore such a one in _a spirit of gentleness_; *each one* looking to yourself, so that you too will not be tempted. [2] Bear one another's burdens, and thereby fulfill the law of Christ. [3] For if anyone thinks he is something when he is nothing, he deceives himself. [4] But each one must _examine his own work_, and then he will have *reason for* boasting in regard to himself alone, and _not in regard to another_. [5] For each one will _bear his own load_.

Paul is concluding his message. He acknowledges that there are those reading him who have not caved into the pressure to return to the law or legalistic practices. Those who are walking in the Spirit are to be gentle with others. I feel a pang of conviction here because my emotional hot buttons, my trigger points, are engaged with religious leaders. It's just deep in my heart. And even the hierarchy that flows down the line gets me pumped up.

That's my flesh kicking in. Yet, I intellectually see that gentleness and kindness are some of the fruit of the Spirit. My tendency has been to be discouraged when failing in this area, yet I know I will grow in being gentler and kinder.

As Paul says here, we are to examine ourselves, our own "work" and not to compare ourselves to others. We are complex people and we have years of relationships that may be healthy or strained. It all has an influence on our responses today. I will simply say that I'm a work in progress, and that is not an easy position for me to consider with my all-or-nothing thinking.

> ⁶ The one who is *taught the word* is to *share all good things* with the one who *teaches him*. ⁷ Do not be deceived, God is not mocked; for whatever a man *sows*, this he will also *reap*. ⁸ For the one who *sows* to his own *flesh* will from the *flesh* reap *corruption*, but the one who *sows to the Spirit* will from the Spirit reap *eternal life*. ⁹ *Let us* not lose heart in doing good, for in due time we will reap if we do not grow weary. ¹⁰ So then, while we have opportunity, *let us do good to all people, and especially to those who are of the household of the faith*.

And here is encouragement to sow to the Spirit, which I read as walk in the Spirit.

The other imperative Paul leaves us with is the call to "do good to all people" and this is congruent with the idea of "love everyone, always." When we teach about those "in" and "out" of the faith, there's a subtle message that we have it figured out and that others are "less than" until they join in our particular faith. Intellectually, we don't agree with that notion, but the seeds are planted in our minds.

Paul's imperative is to love everyone. Yes, he adds, "especially to those who are of the household of the faith." Yet do not miss that we are to love everyone. When I adopt this attitude, anyone can become a member of the household of the faith, now or in the future. Therefore, I read this message as one of loving people. The more I'm walking in the Holy Spirit and allowing the fruit of the Spirit to flow through me, the more I and those around me will benefit.

> ¹¹ See with what _large letters_ I am writing to you with my own hand. ¹² Those who desire to make a _good showing in the flesh_ try to _compel you_ to be _circumcised_, simply so that they will _not be persecuted_ for the cross of Christ. ¹³ For those who are circumcised do not even keep the Law themselves, but they _desire to have you circumcised so that_ they may _boast in your flesh_. ¹⁴ But may it never be that I would boast, except in _the cross of our Lord Jesus Christ_, through which the world has been _crucified to me_, and _I to the world_. ¹⁵ For neither is _circumcision anything_, nor _uncircumcision_, but _a new creation_. ¹⁶ And those who _will walk_ by this rule, _peace_ and _mercy be_ upon them, and _upon the Israel of God_.

Paul recognizes some wish to have those to whom he is writing circumcised and have their reasons. He also says that they might avoid persecutions, which are coming from the Jews, not the Romans. The Roman Empire was not interested in whether Jewish Christians were circumcised.

Yet Paul is teaching that it is about new life, not outward appearances. Paul is writing to implore them to stay with the Spirit, to walk in this new way of life.

Sola Spiritu Ambulatio

¹⁷ From now on let no one cause trouble for me, for I bear on my body the brand-marks of Jesus.

¹⁸ The <u>*grace*</u> of our Lord Jesus Christ be with <u>*your spirit*</u>, brethren. Amen.

He concludes with his blessing for grace and the connection to their spirit. This has been a letter about flesh versus Spirit, about law versus freedom, about faith and adherence to tradition. The great lessons in this letter are the origins of the Sixth Sola.

I mentioned earlier that much of our teaching is to zero in on a set of verses and pull them out to make a point. My preference is to capture the flow of the story. What are the concerns? Why is this letter written? Who is writing it? These are not unique "Bible study" principles, but in my 40 years, the Bible has been treated like a manual.

No Longer A Prescription Medicine

The Scriptures are written by men, who have their own history and experiences which influence their thought processes. When we make statements like, "inerrant Word of God" and "inspired Word of God" and then pull only a verse here and a verse there, we are losing the context. My intention here is to share the flow of what Paul is expressing.

Thus far, the book of Acts has formed the basis for asking, "what is God up to?" Now here, it's Paul's address to the Galatian people. What I have presented are brief snapshots, if you will, of how I read a chapter a day and consider what the Scripture is speaking to me about and the flow of the message that is coming through.

I don't read Galatians as a standalone book; I review how this was where Paul first took the gospel into this region and there was the Jewish and Gentile issue of circumcision, which was thought to be managed with a letter from the leaders in Jerusalem, but we see that it was not. Thanks for hanging in with me on the amount of Scripture reading. It demonstrates some of my methodology and my thought process.

Next, I wish to see what connection we may have between the last 500 years of Reformation and my proposal to focus the next 500 years on our own transformation. The first move in our relationships would not be to reform others, but to consider in what loving way we may interact. Some call for revival within the church; my view is if we all focus on transformation and ask the Holy Spirit to bring out the fruit out of each of us, only then will revival come. I believe in you all. We can lift the weights. We got this, right?

CHAPTER 9

LUTHER LEADS WITH REFORMATION: I LEAD WITH TRANSFORMATION

It's 2020 and we recently celebrated the 500th anniversary of the 95 Theses that Martin Luther nailed to the Wittenberg Church door. It's a milestone in history. Most scholars and historians would say this is the beginning of the Reformation. Yet we also know that Martin Luther was in process. He was not a finished product.

The story goes that Martin was not yet fully embracing a "born again" faith in 1517. He was not happy with the organized religious order of his time. The 95 Theses were not a path to a better way, but a rant against all the things he saw as wrong. For the especially ambitious readers, you may want to find a list of the Theses. If you can read German, great, otherwise find an English version or use Google translate.

I did this a few years back and thought, "Wow, there are many specific complaints that are no longer relevant." We love to mention the 95 Theses and yet, it was more symbolic than about content. I was aiming to finish and publish *The Sixth Sola* back in 2017, but it was not ready. It also was mostly an expression of grievances.

I continued to work at this Sixth Sola, the Spiritu Ambulatio. I do ask myself quite frequently whether I am practicing what I'm preaching. If I were, I sense that my emotions and relationships would be far superior than they happen to be. It's quite discouraging to be formulating a better way and at the same time not seeing it totally manifest in your own life. Recently, I'm coming to a crossroads. It's one thing to work these out on our own, it's another to explode with "results" in our lives and I suspect, that it will only happen when I am engaged with others in living a Spiritu Ambulatio life.

Mindset of Reformation vs. Transformation

This is a point to repeat, which the collective Christian community has studied for more than 500 years. The emphasis is often on outward reforms, and my one thesis is that we would be better to encourage each other during the next 500 years to transform. Others are already doing it. Indeed, it's been going on for 2,000 years. My observation is that the fracturing of the church over the last 500 years continues as we seek the ultimate Reformed organization with which to proceed. Let's flip this around, "own" our personal transformation, and find those around us who wish to do the same.

It is not a judgment of who is doing better. Remember "What Is That To You? You Follow Me!" There are no comparisons. The mystery of the Great Relationship is between each of us and God. It is beyond mediators. This is how I wish to kick off this Luther/Ward connection. Reformation/Transformation.

It is a bit humorous for me to stack myself up with Martin Luther. But why not? He's "just a dude." Apparently, he made fun of Copernicus for suggesting that the planets orbited the sun and commented that scientists always have to come up with a new idea. Gee, Martin, do you think Sola Scriptura and Sola Fide were a bit new? How about a Roman Catholic monk marrying? Yeah, a real trendsetter. Plus, I lived in Berlin from 1993 to 1998 and that was four years after the Berlin Wall came down, so early scenes of Wittenberg were pretty ugly.

What I am getting at is, Martin was an "old dude" in a painting from 500 years ago, but on God's timeline, he was walking in the Spirit and did not "name it that" and he could have argued with Erasmus that you want to "choose"? Go ahead, choose to walk in the Holy Spirit. I suspect Martin would get a chuckle about all that's happened in the last 500 years, and yet our "book" is the same. I'm just finding the next Sola for the next 500 years. That's all.

The flow of events presented by Luke in Acts, and then Paul's own letter to the Galatians describes the early church progressing from a divided Jewish community to one that includes Gentiles. This eventually leads to the integration of these two groups. The struggle of whether to circumcise or not was the debate that Paul and Barnabas were working out with Peter, John, and James. Paul poses the choice of whether we are going to follow our flesh or walk in the Spirit.

This may or may not have completely resolved itself at that time. It's more likely that it continued, and quite possibly continues to this day with other boundary markers taking the place of circumcision. The classic examples have been: no smoking, dancing, drinking, etc. When these are in place, the presence of God is not the key. Instead, following legalism becomes the focus and we lose all the joy and abundant life that Jesus himself called us to enjoy.

Is there a solution that would give us the perfect church?

Spiritual Gifts

We all have spiritual gifts. One noteworthy passage on this topic can be found in 1 Corinthians 12. Paul is writing to the Corinthian church, a community in which he spent more than 18 months.

Paul writes,

> [12] Now concerning _spiritual gifts_, brethren, I do not want you to be unaware. [2] You know that when you were pagans, *you were* led astray to the mute idols, however you were led. [3] Therefore I make known to you that no one speaking by the Spirit of God says, "Jesus is accursed"; and no one can say, "Jesus is Lord," except by _the Holy Spirit_.

Paul begins with gifts, and desires that everyone understand that they come through the Holy Spirit. And if someone says, "Jesus is Lord," then they are gifted!

⁴ Now there are *varieties of gifts*, but *the same Spirit*. ⁵ And there are varieties of ministries, and the same Lord. ⁶ There are varieties of effects, but the same God who works all things in all *persons*. ⁷ But *to each one* is given *the manifestation of the Spirit* for the common good. ⁸ For to one is given *the word of wisdom* through the Spirit, and to another *the word of knowledge* according to the same Spirit; ⁹ to another *faith* by the same Spirit, and to another *gifts of healing* by the one Spirit, ¹⁰ and to another the *effecting of miracles*, and to another *prophecy*, and to another the *distinguishing of spirits*, to another *various kinds of tongues*, and to another the *interpretation of tongues*. ¹¹ But *one and the same Spirit* works all these things, *distributing to each* one individually just as He wills.

Each of us has a gift—each one. Here, Paul lists several. For sake of clarity, what might we infer from this list, considering these are inerrant writings of Paul's from 2,000 years ago to the Corinthian church? Take the next step and continue to ask about the Holy Spirit today and how these gifts may show up.

The Word of Wisdom

The English translation does not use "words" of wisdom, but singular "word," which indicates that the Holy Spirit is revealing wisdom. In particular, this wisdom arises in thoughts, strategies, and plans that are wise for those who are possessed of this gift and for themselves and for the people in their community. They may be excellent sources to be consulted when faced with a challenging decision. As Paul was traveling through various regions, he was with several others with various gifts. It is not unlikely that one of them, whether Luke, Timothy, or Silas, may have had this gift.

The Sixth Sola

The Word of Knowledge

Again, notice not "words," but "word."

Knowledge is a gift looking for an application. Knowledge may be built and be in waiting until needed. Yet someone expressing knowledge, truth, may inspire action simply by connecting what worked in the past and visualizing how it may be acted on in the present and future. Someone may make a comment that comes from a place of study, research, and that word may inform choices for the future.

Faith

I would imagine the gift of faith, or those with a gift of faith, would have a vision for themselves. By that, I mean they would be in touch with what God is calling them to do. We know that we are all called to take hold of faith, and that faith is the foundation for knowing that God has chosen us to be in his Kingdom.

This gift of faith may show up in those who have a vision, perhaps of something that has not been done before. Given that, it is not unlikely that these people would be viewed as risk takers. They sense a call to some activity that is not happening at the moment but see in it a new way that may run "against the grain" while actually being the best way forward.

Healing

Healing may be negatively influenced by public displays and media about events. But when one experiences healing in those closest to them, or they themselves, it is a convincing experience that others may deny. But to the person healed, it is true. There are those carrying out a ministry of healing. Eric Metaxas's show features "Miracle Mondays," and his book *Miracles* documents others' experiences. What's more, did we not just read of healings? Peter and John say, "silver and gold I do not have, but what I do have is the power of God, get up and walk…" From Acts 4. And the man is healed.

He's quite pleased with the results. He's leaping! And yet, the leaders don't want to believe, the want to stop it. Why not be thankful, why the interrogation over the healing? Do we not have much to be healed from? Does your church have someone with the gift of healing?

There are physical healings, and yet perhaps more than ever we can use healing with emotional pain and suffering. Counseling ministries are in this space and bring great relief for those suffering from trauma.

Miracles

What, then, is a miracle? Should we include health and healing? Perhaps, but what else? Are non-bodily changes miracles? When Peter, John, and Paul are let out of prison by an angel, that's a miracle. Do we have examples of miracles being worked through people?

When Philip is transported after speaking with the Ethiopian eunuch, that's a miracle. But did Philip have the gift? Or was it simply the action of the Holy Spirit? What would a person who has this gift look like today?

Would they be aware of a challenge that seemingly had no solution from vantage point of wisdom or knowledge? And would they be able to forge a way forward that relies solely on the power of God? When Paul tells the sailors not to kill anyone so that they may all safely reach shore, is that the gift of miracles working through Paul? It appears to be more miracle than wisdom.

The examples are more of the living God intervening, and yet they have come through Paul, Peter, and John in many cases. Circumstances on this planet change from day-to-day; we are tested to accept unavoidable suffering and celebrate great joy of relief.

Prophecy

In Judaism, the prophets operated under the Law. There are books on this subject. My intent in writing this is to direct us toward transformation.

We may have outsourced prophecy to the professional seminary graduate who has the schooling to read Greek and Hebrew and get the right answers. The typical American Protestant church hires a pastor to bring that message and be the reason folks come to services on Sunday morning.

They are "gifted orators" and most are serving in a great way. They have raised the bar on how to communicate. Yet, we are missing the fact that the voice of God also speaks through less-gifted orators, like Paul himself!

Churches have members in their bodies that have the gift of prophecy, and they are not being heard due to the organizational structures that don't encourage other voices. It comes across as if they protect the harmony and common beliefs, as opposed to allowing others to speak and see if an alternative view may be helpful to others in the form of more inclusivity.

My drive for more inclusion is impacted by my lack of interest in harmony. For me, having different views on just about everything is fine. In fact, the items we tend to debate and separate ourselves on, such as culture, politics, even religious doctrines, are not core to the reconciliation that God brought us. Therefore, I do not have an issue with not being harmonious, and that comes out as contentious and contrarian only to those that want to impose a base of harmony on tradition.

Thus, I am frequently misunderstood. Sorry, but if you have reached this far and are looking for a harmonious view, it's not here. I am about inclusion. We need to love God and love people first. There is too much being "right" going on. That's my prophetic word, my call to walk in the Spirit, not in knowledge and accuracy about Jesus.

Distinguishing of Spirits

In 1 John, the distinguishing of spirits is named as something that's very important, and yet John's message to a body or a church is that we can do it. We often read these words as if they were addressed to individuals, but there's no reason not to consider a slight reframing such that we hear it as a call to a real body that would rely on mutual support.

1 John 4:1–3

⁴ Beloved, do not believe *every spirit*, but test the spirits to see whether they are from God, because many false prophets have gone out into the world. ² By this you know <u>*the Spirit*</u> of God: <u>*every spirit*</u> that confesses that Jesus Christ has come in the flesh is from God; ³ and every spirit that does not confess Jesus is not from God; this is the *spirit* of the antichrist, of which you have heard that it is coming, and now it is already in the world.

Tongues and Interpretation of Tongues

Of all the gifts, this one seems to have the most controversy.

The manifestation of the Holy Spirit in Acts 2 was through "tongues of fire." The dispersed Jews returned to Jerusalem for celebrations, such as Shavuot, the giving of the Law on tablets, 50 days after Passover.

For me, speaking in "tongues" is a switch. I speak German (not perfectly, but fairly well) and yet it's not what the church considers speaking in tongues. It is often considered a prayer language that people don't recognize from our known languages. All the same, it is possible that there are those that do speak in tongues.

This was a brief overview, but there are other lists of spiritual gifts. My purpose is not to write a definitive explanation of these gifts, as it is up to each of us to determine where God is calling us and which gifts He is bringing forth in our being, soul, mind, and spirit. Let's grow in acknowledging the power in the Holy

Spirit, and with what Paul describes as a body. Let's help each other discover our gifts, because it is part of loving one another, and then celebrate the gifts of others.

Paul returns to the one body.

¹² For even as *the body is one* and *yet* has many members, and all the members of the body, though they are many, are *one body*, so also is Christ. ¹³ For by *one Spirit* we were all *baptized into one body*, whether Jews or Greeks, whether slaves or free, and we were all made to drink of *one Spirit*.

Oneness: Harmony vs. Inclusivity

How is our oneness working today? Do we know what it looks like? Is it fine to have multiple "beliefs" or might that be confusing? We have a message of one God and one body, yet we have so many varieties that make me uncomfortable, I don't know about you. Perhaps I have it wrong. My heart says we are mad for more unity.

To salvage the situation, one could argue that over time, people have created and grown their organizations based on core principles and standards that are different from other denominations. Yet, in many urban environments, with 15 to 30 churches of various denominations, how would one choose? Should we be choosing in the first place? I suppose it's cynically become a brand management activity.

If we are going to continue to elevate the importance of our doctrines, beliefs, and structures to carry out what we believe is in the Scripture for all of us, then at minimum, every church should strive to acknowledge that the Holy Spirit has brought people with various gifts together in a spiritual community. The variety of gifts would ideally be manifested in each local body. More importantly, as a member of the community, employing each person's gift will not only serve the community, but bring the Great Relationship its daily expression.

Personal transformation is a start to improving our communities. And quite possibly, my family experience is likely why I have come to not "believe" in denominations and have "trust" issues with organized religion. And don't discount that I "need to move on from my past"; I get it. But our pasts shape how God can use us in our callings. If Joseph wasn't sold into slavery, then the Exodus would not be set up.

The "counselors" in Joseph's prison may tell him to "just get over it" and perhaps he did, as he didn't let it not continue in faith.

In the USA, many comment that there are many "dropping out" of organized religion, and look at the statistics confirming this truth. I sense that it is not that people are losing faith in God, but that people are not satisfied with their "experience." And those who are still in the organized churches who have found that "it works for them" may think that those leaving are giving up.

I don't have an answer for the organizations. I have a snarky view that the churches may be like Blockbuster Video being replaced by Netflix. Only in this case, the Holy Spirit is Netflix. Christians may wish to continue with their congregations. My desire is that whether you stay, go, or join some other organization, that you get in the gym.

We Do Not Have To Wait For Anyone Else

This is about what's called the Spiritual Disciplines, and yet for me that even sounds too highbrow. I subtly call this Spiritu Ambulatio, not because I want to be thought of as "intelligent" but a bit of thumbing my nose at intelligentsia. Did not the son of man simply "hang out" with sinners, tax collectors, prostitutes? Was he arguing with them? My recollection is he loved them. He was a bit upset with those that thought they had it all figured out. And perhaps there are many leaving, as the continuous virtue signal to "do more" is wearing thin.

It's quite possible we will do more when we are finding our callings, our purpose, and then serve in the power that God himself provides. Doesn't that come across better than being a scholar? Having the knowledge? Yes, it's more love.

Someone asked me what this might look like. It might be as simple as waking up in the morning, getting a reminder that God is present, reading a chapter, journaling our thoughts, reflecting on our circumstances and our season in life, then taking that presence with us all day long into every interaction with others and with our own thoughts.

Also, there is power in seeking others who wish to assist us in areas of our weaknesses and bolster others' areas with where we are stronger. But there has to be a shared vision and purpose. We need to end the virtue signaling that certain activities are more meaningful than others. Every activity is meaningful when we walk in the Spirit: smiling when filling the tank with gasoline or realizing that charging the battery is an expression of God's love for his creation. We have 7 billion opportunities to share love, so let's get to it.

The Sixth Sola

What Can We Do?

As I was deciding whether to put out a book on my frustrations with organized religion and how it may be another 500-year expression of dissatisfaction, I shifted to what is a positive transformative way to proceed. It's easy to point out and critique what's not quite right, but what can I move toward—that's how the Spiritu Ambulatio took shape. I hesitated to let others know I was considering writing this book, and once I did, one friend was interested. Listening and thinking this message was meaningful to me, he encouraged me to pursue finishing this. His support has been instrumental, and he appreciates the Holy Spirit view and that helped me finish what I started.

This is an example of two Imago Dei getting together, not because we "go to the same church" but because we share faith in the one true God. It was refreshing and I probably needed an "outsiders'" point of view. We may have organizations that may not agree, but in a loving way, a human way, the way it was always meant to be, we held each other up with a spirit of respect and love. He's more harmonious than I am, but he accepted and understood that I was not. This is the journey we are on. We both know we can use transformation, and we are heading that way. We are not out to reform others.

For me, because I come from a "we must be right" organized religious network, I have to read this myself and see that "being right" is not the most important. Paul himself acknowledges that he does not know it all.

Ironically, this is the exact verse after the "Man Cards," once again in 1 Corinthians 13:12–13

¹² For now we see in a mirror dimly, but then face to face; now I know in part, but then I will know fully just as I also have been fully known. ¹³ But now faith, hope, love, abide these three; but the greatest of these is love.

I can go on and on. German pastors don't appreciate American fundamentalists bringing the "Gawspuhl" to the Germans as if only Americans have it all figured out. We need to let our identities with these Reformed organizations take a very distant place in the hierarchy of priorities. It is loving others that needs to move. It's right here with Paul: The greatest of these is love. Faith and hope will fade as we enter eternity.

Backing up to more from Paul in 1 Corinthians 12.

¹⁴ For the body is *not one member*, but *many*. ¹⁵ If the foot says, "Because I am not a hand, I am not *a part* of the body," it is not for this reason *any the less a part* of the body. ¹⁶ And if the ear says, "Because I am not an eye, I am not *a part* of the body," it is not for this reason *any the less a part* of the body. ¹⁷ If the whole body were an eye, where would the hearing be? If the whole were hearing, where would the sense of smell be? ¹⁸ But now God has placed the members, *each one of them*, in the body, just as *He desired*. ¹⁹ If they were all one member, where would the body be? ²⁰ But now there are many members, but one body. ²¹ And the eye cannot say to the hand, "I have *no need of you*"; or again the head to the feet, "I have *no need of you*." ²² On the contrary, it is much truer that the members of the body which *seem to be weaker* are necessary; ²³ and those *members* of the body which we deem less honorable, on these we bestow more abundant

honor, and our less presentable members become much more presentable,[24] whereas our more presentable members have no need *of it*. *But God* has *so* composed the body, giving more abundant honor to that *member* which lacked,[25] so that there may be <u>*no division in the body*</u>, but *that* the members may have the same care for one another. [26] And if one member suffers, all the <u>*members suffer*</u> with it; if *one* member is honored, all the members rejoice with it.

Celebration Of Diversity

We know a body is physical and yet Paul is speaking metaphorically. We are many, and we are all important. What does Paul say? Does he say we choose what part of the body we are to play? Or is it as Paul writes, namely that God is placing the member as He desires? Yes, this is what takes place.

You may be a part of the body, a part that God made and chose to fit in with the rest. And yet too often, the body parts with the bigger voices tell you whether you belong. Instead of letting "you be you" and celebrating the Imago Dei, we are forced by the bigger voices to serve in the way that they wish.

One solution is to make sure the message is clear that today, one can perform their spiritual service outside the church. Celebrate the opportunities we have each week to serve, whether in the confines of the church membership or service outside the "religious body."

We are different, yet we ought to encourage one another to follow our respective callings. What is your gift? How can you employ it?

²⁷ Now you are Christ's body, and individually members of it. ²⁸ And God has appointed in the church, first _apostles_, second _prophets_, third _teachers_, then _miracles,_ then gifts of _healings_, _helps_, _administrations,_ various kinds of _tongues_.²⁹ All are not apostles, are they? All are not prophets, are they? All are not teachers, are they? All are not _workers of_ miracles, are they? ³⁰ All do not have gifts of healings, do they? All do not speak with tongues, do they? All do not interpret, do they? ³¹ But _earnestly desire the greater gifts_.

And I show you a _still more excellent way_.

And as Paul writes the words, "still more excellent way," we can look ahead to Chapter 13, and we will read that Paul is putting love ahead of doing/service/sacrifice. My desire is to shift our mindset away from reforming the church, from virtue signaling about great endeavors like as the Great Commission or social justice, to simply walking in the Spirit and following what God/Jesus/the Holy Spirit is calling each of us, as a member of the body, to do. This is the mystery Paul, Peter, John describe for us. These apostles are calling us to live each moment from the point of God's presence. Did we not just read in Acts how the living God is calling the shots?

Twitter, Facebook, Instagram have many positive features, but virtue signaling is not one of them. These lead to comparisons that freeze us with thoughts of inadequacy, where we believe only if we do grandiose activities are we acceptable to God. This has created the image that God is distant and sitting back judging our behavior. Only if we post a picture of us doing something awesome will we be accepted.

My desire is to shift our mindset away from reforming the church, from virtue signaling about great endeavors like as the Great Commission or social justice, to simply walking in the Spirit and following what God/Jesus/the Holy Spirit is calling each of us, as a member of the body, to do.

Be Imitators Of Paul

Now, if you are feeling strongly about any task, please, go do it. But I wish there were more Pauls living today. He kind of just did what he was called to do, and that was the end of it. He didn't even call Timothy to send out missionaries to complete the Great Commission. Did Paul miss the memo? Tweet? Facebook post?

In the next chapter, I present a "workout plan" for how to spend more time in the Word. Instead of throwing open the door to hundreds of weights, saying, "Just get in there and start exercising," it is more like following a routine. As a coach, I'm not "teaching" you what the Scriptures mean; I'm encouraging you to teach yourself. I developed this routine and believe that following it for at least one cycle would deepen the message of walking in the Spirit. I wish to coach others in this effort.

Today, I was reading John 21, the image of the disciples fishing without any results. They were doing what they knew best but came away with nothing. Then Jesus strolled out on the beach. He told them to try another time and they found a huge catch. That spoke to my situation today. I needed to understand that God can bring results. He came to them and provided better results than what they could achieve on their own. Normally, I would focus on the end of the chapter, yet this was my learning. It influenced my heart and reinforced that I need to be walking

Luther Leads With Reformation: I Lead With Transformation

in the Spirit. And the walking in the Spirit is not strenuous; it's a mindset shift.

That's my view on teaching. If you are listening to messages, either online or in person, you may want to ask yourself if you are being taught something or if you are being coached to take action from your gifted position. There are likely several combinations, and I understand it can often be both. Yet, if I'm not lifting any weights, I'm not going to get stronger watching the results of someone else's workout.

Carl Friedrich Gauß

Deutschland

My experience with Germany began in 1993, when I took a job with BMW Rolls-Royce. Yeah, pretty snazzy for a young hot shot engineer. The country reunified after 50 years of being divided. One of the fun things was the colorful money! Here's a story about Carl Friedrich Gauß. Above is a photo of a 10 Deutsche mark note from the mid-1990s. It became a key document in my wallet, worth about 6USD today.

As a student of engineering, and then the Six Sigma quality programs, the Gaussian distribution curve became a tool to describe process variation and quality. You may be most familiar with it from the classroom when the teacher is grading on a curve. It means we don't have an absolute measurement of achievement, but a "relative" measure.

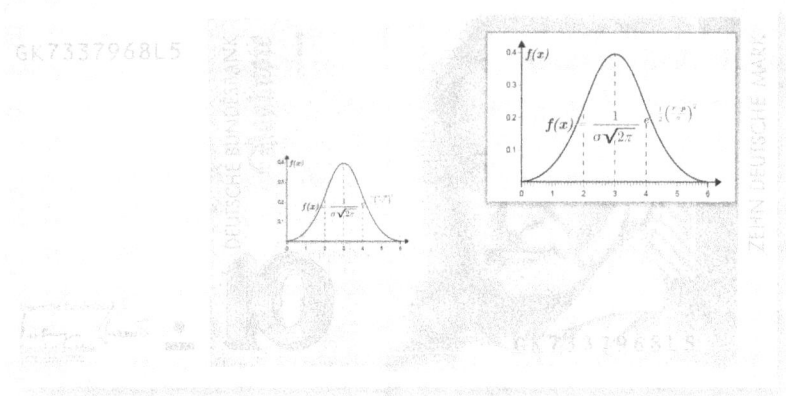

A certain portion of the class would get the As, some would get Bs, and the majority of us would receive Cs. It's a common language we use quite often. This is the simplest description and I do not wish to disrespect Carl, but if the reader is interested in more, there are more articles referencing his mathematical analysis than we could document.

Other uses, perhaps more sophisticated uses of the distribution curves are in manufacturing processes. There are tolerance bounds for what may be called key characteristics. They need to measure a specific amount—not too large and not too small. If we made 100 items, we would like all of them to fit within a range, and the distribution of items in that range might look like this curve.

Moving Beyond The All Or Nothing

As opposed to black and white, all or nothing, a distribution curve visually represents variation and often represents a "total population." For example, if there are 150 million adult males in the United States, and we counted the number of men that measured 5'0" in one-inch increments up to 7'10", we may find the average height of an adult man is 5'10". That's the middle of the curve, with a large number one inch taller and one inch shorter.

The Sixth Sola

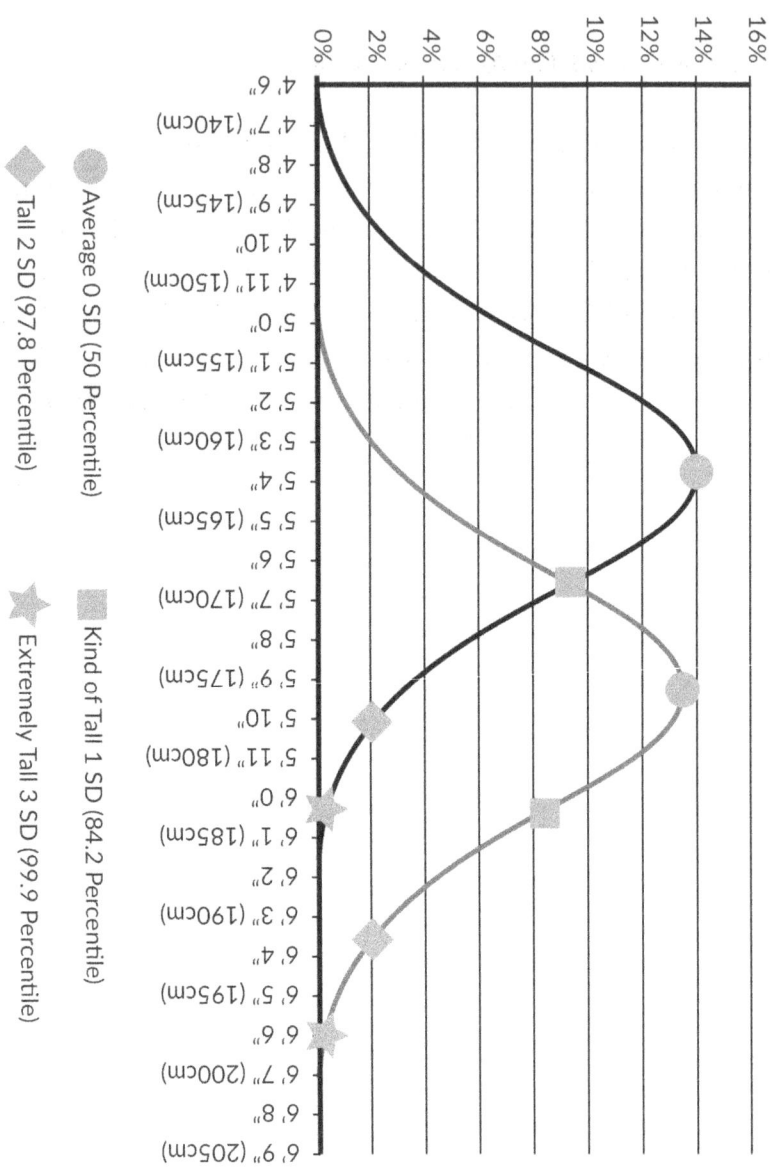

162

I have brought up two concepts: the fruit of the Spirit and spiritual gifts. A distribution curve is useful to demonstrate how both could work.

First, the fruit of the Spirit: We would all like to have more love, joy, peace, patience, kindness, goodness, faithfulness, gentleness, and self-control. When we are introspective, we may find that we struggle with these various fruits of the Spirit. We may be doing well on faithfulness, yet not so well on joy. Coupling walking by the Spirit, a process, with the fruit, you can envision the curve. As I walk by the Spirit, I ask to move to higher levels of joy. I don't become discouraged if I am below average. I consider the joy I have as I walk in the Spirit and ask the Holy Spirit to help me develop more joy in my moment-by-moment living.

If you are confident that you know where you are now with regard to the fruit of the Spirit and believe you are maxed out to the right in outlier performance, excellent. I'm not there. Still, this framework brings a level of encouragement to keep moving. It also allows me to reduce comparisons. Now, I may notice that someone else has much more joy than I. Since this is on the curve, I am not tempted to compare and get discouraged, but to celebrate that they are at a high level. Maybe instead of competing with them, they may have a word of wisdom for me. When am I more likely to listen? If I see it as growth or improvement? Or if I see it as black and white, in which I either have it or I don't?

The Sixth Sola

Fruit of the Spirit - Not The Same Amount Of Each
GOAL Is To Increase

- JOY
- PEACE
- KINDNESS
- SELF-CONTROL
- LOVE
- GENTLENESS
- PATIENCE
- GOODNESS
- FAITHFULNESS

How Shall We View Gifts?

When it comes to spiritual gifts, let's apply the framework. We are likely to have some measure of each of the spiritual gifts. The message I understand Paul to be conveying is that if we have received the Holy Spirit, we will be gifted with a purpose or a calling. There may be elements of our eventual purpose early in our lives. I think of Joseph, who spoke as a very young man of his vision to lead his brothers. He was correct, but he had to endure many years of pain to get to that point. Still, Joseph put the people of Israel in a position for God to perform one of the most significant displays of His love and power.

We have many ways of statistically studying people and their behaviors. Yet our faith says God knows everything about us. Is He not shaping us for His purpose? As for the curve, if we take a population of Christians, it's possible we all have a measure of a particular gift. If we were placed on a curve, we would find most in the middle of the distribution, and then outliers on the upper and lower portions of the curve.

The Sixth Sola

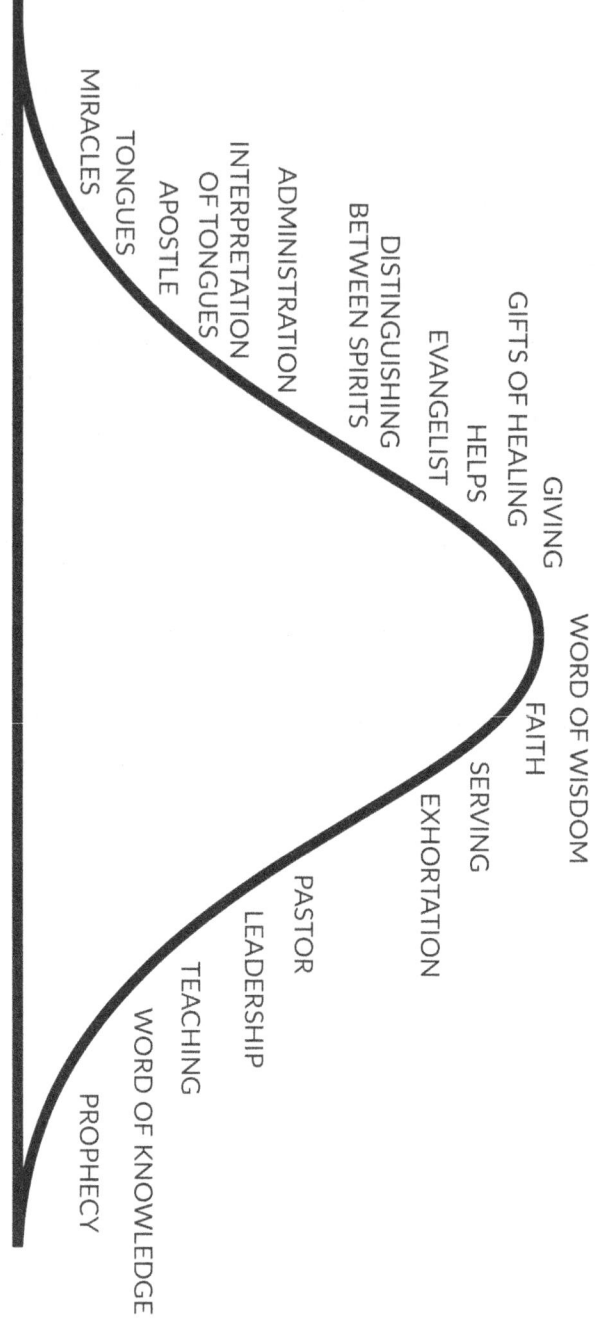

Many Gifts: Determine and Use Your Strongest

Is it not reasonable to believe that walking in the Spirit will bring out our strongest gifts? There may be some churches and organizations that do this well, and they encourage each member to exercise their gifts. And when we are operating here, could this not be where our best modes of service are evident?

Before we move on, let me summarize the discussion to this point. Churches have been and continue to reform. From the Solas of Martin Luther, there is a need to shift our focus to the Holy Spirit and our own personal transformation. Revival is more likely to come when we acknowledge that the Holy Spirit has always been with us, and that each of us shall own our spiritual growth by letting go of the expectations of our church leadership and embracing our individual callings and gifts. When we have people who are called and they do what they are called to do, there's power displayed.

Transformation Is Not Linear

I'm humbled; I have entered the process of transformation. I am likely on the low end in many characteristics of fruit/gifts, and yet, the Spirit may be bringing change. It is not up to me to make it happen, to try harder, but to allow the Word, both written and Holy Spirit, to work a transformation in me. It is not a comparison to others, but a comparison to myself, very much like exercise and fitness is a comparison from where we were, to where we are now. I must continue to walk in the Spirit. Paul has an excellent word from Philippians 1:21–26.

> [21] For to me, _to live is Christ_ and to _die is gain_. [22] But if _I am_ to live _on_ in the flesh, this _will mean fruitful labor for me_; and _I do not know_ which to _choose_. [23] But I am hard-pressed from

both *directions*, having <u>*the desire to depart*</u> and <u>*be with Christ*</u>, for *that* is very much better; ²⁴ yet to <u>*remain on in the flesh*</u> is <u>*more necessary for your sake*</u>. ²⁵ <u>*Convinced*</u> of this, <u>*I know that I will remain and continue with you*</u> all for <u>*your progress*</u> and <u>*joy*</u> in <u>*the faith*</u>, ²⁶ so that <u>*your proud confidence*</u> in me <u>*may abound*</u> in Christ Jesus through <u>*my coming to you again*</u>.

This is Paul's letter to the Philippians, the first people to whom he brought the gospel in northern Greece, Macedonia to be specific. He briefly stayed with them before being pressured to leave for Thessalonica and then Berea. We believe Paul is writing from his prison cell in Rome near the end of his life. And it is more than five and possibly ten years since he first arrived in this city.

We have read these passages often. Paul is living, writing, and proclaiming the gospel with the view that he is serving Christ. That's not an easy concept to understand and take on in our own lives. Still, Paul has been on a 15- to 25-year journey depending on when we start the clock, and he's experiencing this Holy Spirit guide and these open doors for him to proclaim the gospel, see the Holy Spirit, bring a response, and then teach, train, coach the people he came to love. We often simplify Paul as a tough guy dishing out judgment, when most every letter he began with great admiration to those that he recognized as having responded in faith and were smart. They loved people.

Did Paul Not Love Those Of Faith?

He contrasts that with dying and calls the latter gain. He writes that when he dies, and we all do, he is confident that he will eventually resurrect and be with God. He makes a curious statement about not knowing which to choose. I'm not sure Paul would say he has a choice, but this is what he writes.

His view is that if he lives, he will continue fruitful labor in guiding the growth of this mystery of the gospel. This is his contribution in letter and in face-to-face gatherings as beneficial for others' "progress" and "joy" in the faith. And he finishes with his desire to meet with them in person. Is it not possible for all of us to adopt Paul's view? How can we find our spiritual gift and find a way to bring it into service?

Reviewing our path:

- Sola Spiritu Ambulatio (walking in the Spirit)
- For us and others, the question is: "Did you receive the Holy Spirit when you believed?"
- Do we display more fruit of the Spirit in our lives and relationships?
- We are gifted. We have something to say, something to do, and the living God wants to have a Great Relationship with us. As we pursue that Relationship, we will find our purpose and calling.
- A process of daily reading may be helpful to facilitate spiritual growth as we engage with God and the Holy Spirit in our sanctification.

Up to here, in the background, has been my reading plan of what the post-Resurrection, Ascension, and coming of the Holy Spirit has been recorded for us. It may be worth repeating, and I don't write this as an apology but in humility, that I am confessing this is not my opinion but my interpretation of what I have been reading. After coming back to these 151 chapters perhaps 12 times now, I may be hitting Malcolm Gladwell's 10,000 hours.

I mention this because I believe God wants us all to have confidence in His Word, and that Word includes the Holy Spirit as part of the Trinity. And I might be able to pull some verses to defend this opinion, yet I actually think it best if you would enter into reading this word yourself. It's the 21st century and we have so many ways to read and get answers to questions that I recommend engaging with this plan.

CHAPTER 10

THE PLAN AND CALL TO ACTION

Let me explain how this reading plan grew over the course of the last six years. It started with my snarky response to "Man/Resolution Cards" and since I did not trust the summary attached to verses plucked from the Bible, I decided to read for the whole context and to take into account the entire message.

After a few rich experiences with this approach, it was easy to make the decision to read all of Paul's letters in the rough order in which they were written. I did some research to find the proper order. While there is some debate about whether Paul wrote all the letters, and which letter came first, I finally settled on the following list:

Approximate Year	Letter/Book	Chapters
50	James	5
53-55	Galatians	6
53	1 Thessalonians	5
53	2 Thessalonians	3
57	1 Corinthians	16
57	2 Corinthians	13
58	Romans	16
	Four years no writings included	
62	Ephesians	6
62	Philippians	4
62	Colossians	4
63	Philemon	1
63	**Luke**	**24**
64	Acts	28
65	Hebrews	13
65	Titus	3
65	1 Timothy	6
67	2 Timothy	4
67	1 Peter	5
67	**Mark**	**16**
67	**Matthew**	**28**
68	2 Peter	3
68	Jude	1
68	**Revelation**	**22**
85	**John**	**21**
90	1 John	5
92	2 John	1
95	3 John	1
	Reading Program	151
	With Gospels	260

I placed the four Gospels and the book of Revelation in the list. Given this progression, we know Paul was doing the Great Commission without the words in Matthew 28:19-20. We also know that Matthew didn't need to investigate what was happening to record what he witnessed, whereas Luke did have to ask questions. As a result of Luke asking questions of Peter, John, and Paul, the account he records in Acts 1 is more verified than Matthew's independent account. From what we know, he did not consult with anyone else. There are great narratives in Matthew. It is an important Gospel and gives us much to learn, but the Great Commission is not the key message. Still, those two verses have been lifted to the pinnacle of importance.

Am I against missions? No, I repeat. But let's do it through the power of the Holy Spirit as we read the actual working of the Great Commission. If we want to know about how God worked out the Great Commission, we look at the book of Acts, and it's not the unleashing of the gospel, but the unleashing of the Holy Spirit. Too many churches may be stuck in Apollos mode—that's teaching accurately about Jesus but having no real power of the Holy Spirit. We are back to the VIQ, Very Important Question: "Did you receive the Holy Spirit when you believed?" Acts 19:2.

Let's Get Started With The Beginning

In Acts, we see God himself intervening. There was not a continuation of the imperative "go." Why do I devote all these words to this subject? I find this imperative being a virtue signal, guilt-lifting way to garner commitment from an emotional response, usurping the Holy Spirit from calling people to serve. We all are susceptible and influenced by calls to virtue. And yet, we have a Scripture, a savior, that doesn't do that, so why do we?

The Sixth Sola

A personal story: I arrived in Berlin in 1993 and began a relationship with an American missionary and his family's story as they were setting up a church. I would eventually come to learn a sad dramatic history. He told me about 20 years earlier, he was 19 from a fundamentalist church in Georgia. He was sent to Norway with his new bride. He described how he was in a battle for his faith as he brought American cultural Christianity to Norway to save the "spiritually dead" Europeans.

I didn't understand his struggle at the time. It all seemed fantastically odd. But since then I have come to appreciate the pressures, he may have been experiencing with the leadership calling for him to "go." This is oft repeated to those of us sitting in the American pews, but I suspect some are zealously sent out unprepared and often greatly struggle with cultural differences and in some way may fail as a result. Therefore, let's make sure we have our Great Relationship first, before sending others out. Or better yet, just go yourself and we can read about it 2,000 years later.

The Great Commission is the greatest "verse pluck" of all time. Let's get the entire message from the forest before we begin examining the bark on the trees. With that, I set out with Paul, backed up to Acts for context, then added the others. After reviewing the chronological order, some additional information shed light on the writings.

Who Is James Writing To?

For example, the book of James is the earliest. In the very first line, James is writing to the Jewish Christians that were dispersed, likely after Stephen's martyr in Acts 8. With a chronological view, one can see that the entire Gentile and Jew complexity was not debated until many years after James wrote his book. Therefore, reading James with the view that he is writing to Jews who have changed their faith in response to what Jesus had done is an important consideration. This is the inerrant Word of God, and inspired by God, and yet the writers are human and are influenced by what they experience.

They are not perfect; they write from their heart and it's not a magic translation from God's mouth to the writer's pen. It is part of the mystery, and we know there are plenty of debates on these words. I am one who believes it is sufficient to consider them inerrant and inspired by God, yet I don't fully understand the depths of how this is possible.

Backing up a bit, I quickly realized Paul's letters were written to churches and I was not taking advantage of what I could learn from Acts. At one point in the first year, I may have flipped back and forth to specific sections of Acts that discussed the cities to which Paul was writing. I then decided to add the book of Acts to the beginning of the reading plan.

Again, this was not a simple "figure it out" experience. It was a learn by doing. I still listened to messages and podcasts. I tuned into R. C. Sproul on renewing the mind. While most of what I was doing revolved around this reading plan, I was influenced by other Scriptures and external sources.

A few years into this process, I came across one of my favorite passages, "What Is That To You? You Follow Me!" WITTY? YFM! If you struggle with comparing yourself to others, read through John 21 and think of Peter, think of John recording this story. John told us he could have written numerous stories, but he included this one. I think it is so significant. I do see it as the Great Relationship. We need to start here, and so I added this chapter up front. I was at over a hundred chapters, so what was one more? We start here, the direct relationship with God. I can only imagine that the WITTY? YFM! experience was an embarrassing moment for Peter. He just recommitted to "Tend My lambs" and "Shepherd My sheep" and "Tend My sheep," John 21:15–17, only to compare himself to John, and John dutifully recorded this for us all to see. And if we are going to move out on our faith, to be confident in what God is calling us to do, it doesn't have to be anything that anyone else would think is important. That's why this is so great.

> *"What Is That To You? You Follow Me!" WITTY? YFM!*

If we would honor one another, and love people, it may be that the person who does the simplest of jobs is fully walking in the Spirit of God. When we compare, we lose. When we shout from the pulpit, "Some of you are doing jack for Jesus," we are crushing the Spirit of God in His people.

Those statements, virtue signaling comes from pride in that we are doing better than others. WITTY? YFM! ends this, it's your Great Relationship with God. No one can judge. Sure, we may disappoint one another, but as Paul writes for us in 1 Corinthians 4:3–5

> ³ But to me it is a very small thing that I may be examined by you, or by *any* human court; in fact, I do not even examine

myself. **⁴** For _I am conscious of nothing against myself_, yet I am not by this acquitted; but _the one who examines me is the Lord_. **⁵** Therefore do not go on passing judgment before the time but *wait* until the Lord comes who will both bring to light the things hidden in the darkness and disclose the motives of *men's* hearts; and then each man's praise will come to him from God.

Do You Want To Live Confidently?

This is a supreme confidence in our Great Relationship with God. Do you have it? Perhaps like me, you have it sometimes, but not all the time, so let's elevate our confidence in God and let the thoughts of what others might think of our beliefs as a "very small thing." Paul's words don't make us innocent, or acquitted, but it is the Lord that examines us, not anyone of us created beings. Let the confidence rise.

Later, I added John 20. We live in a post-Ascension world, where Pentecost Holy Spirit is present. By that, I mean we know factually that the Romans crucified Jesus. We know that he was resurrected, ascended, and God sent His Holy Spirit. Not even the 12 disciples saw these events coming. This is why it is important to understand this new covenant.

The total number of chapters is now 151. I start fresh with the text in a clean format. No highlights. I copy the text over to another journaling document and integrate current events, circumstances, and roll that into a consideration of how the living God may be speaking to me through this Word. I am sure to review key teachings at least twice each year. I am becoming familiar of where to look and have found some interesting thoughts along the way.

Get It All

This is my "big ask," not just that we read, but that we interact with the Word, make notes, ask questions, and see the overall flow. Many of you have already read and studied these books. My recommendation is to move toward connecting what is happening with the Holy Spirit with your daily life. Make it your devotional. Engage with God through His Word.

I recommend that you make an effort for one week. If you can keep it up, it's like going to the gym. And if you miss a day or two, just come back to where you left off. You can do it. Here's my process.

Methodology and Tools:

- Laptop computer
- Word processing software
- An electronic version of the Bible

We have access to many electronic tools and if you don't have access to copy and paste features, it may require printing out copies and using highlighters and even that may bring a different thought to your mind. It's not how I have been working through this.

For one, I enjoy typing. I created a document with the *New American Standard Bible* and the chapters in the order that I will read them. I find this best and I will only follow this process in this manner because it works for me.

If you do not have access to laptop and electronics, you can still use a Bible, however as I mentioned, you can be creative and possibly print out one chapter individually. I also seek to remove all extraneous information from study Bibles, with cross references and commentary. My opinion is God would not make His Scripture so complicated that we could not understand it without knowing every cultural nuance at the time. That's for another purpose, this is for us to get ourselves walking in the Spirit. Is that the message of this all? You can find out for yourself, read it!

Another reason I prefer electronics is that I am not reminded and clouded by my 40 years of experience working with printed Bibles and seeing Matthew, Mark, Luke, and John followed by Acts, Romans, and Corinthians. That's the order for someone's good reason, but it's not for my reason. If one knows little to nothing of the faith, starting with what Jesus did is logically the best way. I'm assuming the reader is very familiar with the Bible, both the New and Old Testaments.

Going Old School Will Take Creativity

If you use a printed Bible, I suggest you follow along with my description of the electronic version, and then adapt to possibly print chapters and use colored pens, highlighters, and a journal. There are endless creative adaptions to what I am about to share. People will likely amaze me with how they make this process their own.

The important message is we are going to read what was happening after Jesus resurrected and ascended, and how the Holy Spirit and God Himself intervened, and then ask how this mystery of the Holy Spirit may enter our life today. This is why I consider myself not a teacher, but a coach who helps you engage with the Word and the Holy Spirit.

Electronic Method

I start with John 20. I make a journal entry with the date, the time, and a few introductory comments. I might journal on what happened that particular day or the day before if I see a relationship or a behavior that's related to the process of transformation I'm undertaking.

With the electronic text of John 20, I begin, and as I read, I highlight words that trigger my mind in some way. If there are many words that I'm highlighting, I may have 10 words in a phrase or sentence and then I may underline a few words to have that stand out even more. Here's what my John 20 looked like yesterday.

> [20] Now on the first *day* of the week Mary Magdalene came early to the tomb, while it was still dark, and saw <u>*the stone already*</u> taken away from the tomb. [2] So she ran and came to <u>*Simon Peter*</u> and to <u>*the other disciple whom Jesus loved*</u>, and said to them, "<u>*They*</u> have taken away the Lord out of the tomb, and we do not know where they have laid Him." [3] So <u>*Peter*</u> and <u>*the other disciple went forth*</u>, and they were going to the tomb. [4] The two were running together; and the other disciple <u>*ran ahead faster*</u> than Peter and came to the tomb first; [5] and stooping and looking in, he saw the linen wrappings lying *there*; but he <u>*did not go in*</u>. [6] And so Simon Peter also came, following him, and <u>*entered the tomb*</u>; and he *saw the linen wrappings lying *there*, [7] and the face-

cloth which had been on His head, not lying with the linen wrappings, but rolled up in a place by itself. ⁸ So the _other disciple_ who had first come to the tomb then _also entered_, and _he saw and believed_. ⁹ For _as yet they did not understand the Scripture_, that He must _rise again_ from _the dead_. ¹⁰ So the disciples _went away_ again to their own homes.

¹¹ _But Mary was standing outside the tomb weeping_; and so, as _she wept_, she stooped and looked into the tomb; ¹² and she saw _two angels_ in white sitting, one at the head and one at the feet, where the body of Jesus had been lying. ¹³ And they said to her, "_Woman, why are you weeping?_" She said to them, "_Because they have taken away my Lord, and I do not know where they have laid Him._"¹⁴ When she had said this, she turned around and saw Jesus standing _there_, and _did not know that it was Jesus_. ¹⁵ Jesus said to her, "_Woman, why are you weeping? Whom are you seeking?_" _Supposing Him_ to be _the gardener_, she said to Him, "_Sir, if you have carried Him away, tell me where you have laid Him, and I will take Him away._" ¹⁶ Jesus said to her, "_Mary!_" She turned and said to Him in Hebrew, "_Rabboni!_" (which means, Teacher). ¹⁷ Jesus said to her, "_Stop clinging to Me, for I have not yet ascended to the Father; but go to My brethren and say to them, 'I ascend to My Father and your Father, and My God and your God.'_"¹⁸ _Mary Magdalene_ came, announcing to the disciples, "_I have seen the Lord_," and _that_ He had said these things to her.

¹⁹ So when it was _evening on that day_, the first _day_ of the week, and when the _doors were shut_ where the disciples were, for _fear of the Jews_, Jesus came and _stood in their midst_ and said to them, "_Peace be with you._" ²⁰ And when He had said this, He

showed them *both His hands and His side*. The disciples then rejoiced when they saw the Lord. ²¹ So Jesus said to them again, "*Peace be with you; as the Father has sent Me, I also send you*." ²² And when He had said this, He breathed on them and said to them, "*Receive the Holy Spirit*. ²³ *If you forgive the sins of any, their sins have been forgiven them; if you retain the sins of any, they have been retained*."

²⁴ But Thomas, one of the twelve, called Didymus, was not with them when Jesus came. ²⁵ So the other disciples were saying to him, "*We have seen the Lord!*" But he said to them, "*Unless I see in His hands the imprint of the nails, and put my finger into the place of the nails, and put my hand into His side, I will not believe.*"

²⁶ *After eight days* His disciples were again inside, and Thomas with them. Jesus came, the *doors having been shut*, and stood in their midst and said, "*Peace be with you*." ²⁷ Then He said to Thomas, "*Reach here with your finger, and see My hands; and reach here your hand and put it into My side; and do not be unbelieving, but believing*." ²⁸ Thomas answered and said to Him, "*My Lord and my God!*" ²⁹ Jesus said to him, "*Because you have seen Me, have you believed? Blessed are they who did not see, and yet believed*."

³⁰ Therefore many other signs Jesus also performed in the presence of the disciples, which are *not written in this book*; ³¹ but these have been written so that *you may believe that Jesus is the Christ*, the Son of God; and that *believing you may have life in His name*.

The Read-Through

This may be 10 minutes of reading. As I'm reading and adding highlights, I'm letting my mind engage with the Word. I am asking myself, "How is this related to my life? Is there something here for me to consider?" I do this on a laptop. I find a comfortable chair and when I travel, I may even do this on a flight.

These are your experiences and your thoughts on how you are walking in the Spirit and how you relate to people you meet during the day.

After I do the first pass, or as I call it a "read-through," I may take a break. It may be 15 minutes before I come back to it. Or if I'm ready, I move directly into what I call a breakdown. I have read through the chapter, and I've highlighted words and phrases that initially jump out in my mind. This time as I read through, I enter a new line when I start a new sentence, hit a highlighted word or a highlighted underlined word.

The messaging begins to come out. The words begin to form blocks of thoughts, ones that I may note to myself or comment on if there is something related to my current circumstances or relationships.

The Breakdown

Here's how this would look from the breakdown:

[20] Now on the first *day* of the week
<u>Mary Magdalene</u> came early to the tomb, while it was still dark, and saw
<u>the stone already</u> taken away from the tomb. [2]

So
<u>she ran</u> and came to
<u>Simon Peter</u> and to
<u>the other disciple</u>
<u>whom Jesus loved</u>, and said to them,

"<u>They</u> have taken away the Lord out of the tomb, and we do not know where they have laid Him." ³

My comments: (Here it is, John, the disciple whom Jesus loved….So?)

<u>Peter</u>
and
<u>the other disciple</u>
<u>went forth</u>, and they were going to the tomb. ⁴

My comments: Notice John writing this gospel. He doesn't refer to himself as "I" or "me" but in a third-person way as "the other disciple."

The two were running together; and the other disciple <u>ran ahead faster</u> than Peter and came to the tomb first; ⁵ and stooping and looking in, he *saw the linen wrappings lying *there*; but he <u>did not go in</u>. ⁶

My comments: Here, John runs faster than Peter. There's a fact. Better athlete! And more reverent…still just the "other disciple."

And so Simon Peter also *came, following him, and
<u>entered the tomb</u>; and he *saw the linen wrappings lying *there*, ⁷ and the face-cloth which had been on His head, not lying with the linen wrappings, but rolled up in a place by itself. ⁸

So the
<u>other disciple</u> who had first come to the tomb then
<u>also entered</u>, and
<u>he saw and believed</u>. ⁹

For
<u>as yet</u>
<u>they</u>
<u>did not</u>
<u>understand</u>
<u>the Scripture</u>, that He must
<u>rise again</u> from
<u>the dead</u>. ¹⁰

My comments: John states that this was HIS moment of belief/faith, not sure about Peter.

So the disciples
<u>went away</u> again to their own homes.

¹¹ <u>But Mary was standing outside the tomb weeping</u>; and so, as <u>she wept</u>, she stooped and looked into the tomb; ¹² and she *saw
<u>two angels</u> in white sitting, one at the head and one at the feet, where the body of Jesus had been lying. ¹³

And they said to her,

"<u>Woman, why are you weeping?</u>"

She said to them,

"<u>Because they have taken away my Lord, and I do not know where they have laid Him.</u>"[14]

When she had said this, she turned around and *saw <u>Jesus</u> standing *there*, and <u>did not know that it was Jesus</u>. [15]

Jesus said to her,

"<u>Woman, why are you weeping? Whom are you seeking?</u>"

<u>Supposing Him</u> to be <u>the gardener</u>, she *said to Him,

My comments: The GARDENER!! We can "miss" seeing Jesus like Mary. Let's have life today!

Some days, I may dig deeper. I go through the same chapters at least every four to five months. Quite often, some other teaching will catch my attention the next reading. And this is why it's not about my teaching anyone or giving the "right" interpretation. I'm saying, lift the weights. We will all benefit from our efforts.

I record the start time and the end time and make a note of the duration. It's a kick start for the day—a reminder that God's presence is with us, always, everywhere, whether I recognize Him or not. With daily practice, I am moving in a better place. There's no magic formula from practice, and yet, it is such a habit now that I have not stopped. It influences relationships and how I might pray for others. It is all growing in my own Great Relationship as I face my own WITTY? YFM! moments.

It Is All You, The Word, And The Holy Spirit

Because I'm not listening to a message brought to me based on the best "commentaries" seminaries can buy, I engage my mind in how I interact with the Word. The Gardner is a humorous story. Later in the day, I had a free moment to recall this reading. I asked myself, "How did John know that Mary thought Jesus was the Gardner?"

We often read these chapters, but we don't ask questions, your questions, not those handed to you by another person. There are popular devotionals, Brother Lawrence, Oswald Chambers, and others. But here, I am sharing with you about how you and your life are a devotional. You can bring this Word right into your life and ask questions like, "How did John know that Mary thought Jesus was the Gardner?" It's rather humorous just to think that she did, but can John read Mary's mind?

Remember, these are books written by people. Wouldn't we be speaking of a person like this? I imagine at some point Mary was embarrassingly laughing and commenting, "John, you realize I thought Jesus was just the gardener. Can you believe that? Is that not the craziest thing?"

The Sixth Sola

So that's my hypothesis for how John came to write that Mary thought Jesus was the gardener.

And finally, how is this connected to walking in the Spirit, the Sola Spiritu Ambulatio?

As I follow the events, the Holy Spirit has a very frequent appearance. After a few cycles of this, I decided to search the words, "Holy Spirit" and "Spirit" and "spiritual." I was shocked by how frequently these appeared. I created a table to see which chapters are especially meaningful to me as I read through them.

An Aha Moment

I've used the chart below to show where the "Spirit" shows up. I should ask you before you look. Do you think it is more than 25 percent of the chapters? Don't look, but is it over or under 25 percent?

The Plan and Call to Action

CHAPTERS

Book	#	1	2	3	4	5	6	7	8	9	10	11	12	13	14	15	16	17	18	19	20	21	22	23	24	25	26	27	28
John	2																												
Acts	28	SP	SP		SP	SP	SP	SP	SP	SP	SP	SP		SP		SP	SP	SP	SP	SP	SP	SP		SP					SP
Galatians	6			SP	SP	SP	SP																						
1 Thessalonians	5	SP	SP		SP	SP																							
2 Thessalonians	3		SP																										
1 Corinthians	16		SP	SP	SP	SP	SP	SP			SP		SP		SP	SP	SP												
2 Corinthians	13	SP	SP	SP	SP	SP	SP	SP				SP	SP	SP															
Romans	16	SP	SP		SP	SP	SP	SP	SP	SP	SP	SP	SP		SP	SP	SP												
Ephesians	6	SP	SP	SP	SP	SP	SP																						
Philippians	4	SP	SP	SP	SP																								
Colossians	4	SP	SP	SP	SP																								
Philemon	1	SP																											
Hebrews	13	SP	SP	SP	SP		SP			SP	SP		SP	SP															
Titus	3			SP																									
1 Timothy	6			SP	SP	SP	SP																						
2 Timothy	4	SP			SP																								
	130																												
James	5		SP	SP	SP	SP																							
1 Peter	5	SP	SP	SP	SP	SP																							
2 Peter	3	SP																											
Jude	1	SP																											
1 John	5			SP	SP	SP																							
2 John	1																												
3 John	1																												

SP	SPIRIT

189

Well, I was surprised to find that 68 percent of these post-Resurrection writings mention Spirit, Holy Spirit, spirit, spiritual. To me, that's significant. In your faith journey, is the concept of the Holy Spirit at the forefront of your mind? Or could it be you are influenced by those that wish to teach accurately about Jesus and may not really have received the Holy Spirit? I will create a location on my website www.6thsola.com if anyone wishes to comment on how that question is going over with their faith community.

This is the nuts and bolts of it. You have the book, you can create your own electronic versions, or you can visit my website www.6thsola.com and download tools for your own use.

This is why I consider myself not a teacher, but a coach who helps you engage with the Word and the Holy Spirit.

This all seems simple to me, I've been doing some form of this for nearly seven years now. If you would actually give an effort to get into a spiritual gym, you will see "results" and by that I mean, confidence in your Great Relationship, clarity on your calling, a framework to discuss better relationships with yourself and others.

Ask the Holy Spirit to be with you in your moment-by-moment living. Perhaps you will see increased love, joy, fruit. Perhaps you will move closer to a calling that has been placed in your soul. I'm not teaching anything here. I am simply saying, read our Scriptures. You are teaching yourself. I'm here to coach, I'm a guide.

The Hero Redux

You are the hero. You have amazing challenges in your life that I have no idea what you are up against. But I want to reframe this Christian faith, experience, obedience, as a walk in the Spirit. I remind us that we have the Guide. That's what Jesus promised. The Spirit is the Guide. Embrace the power God offers you in the Holy Spirit. It does sound odd and the way I grow in this process is to grind out reading like going to the gym.

When I started this reading plan, I simply wanted to read in the context Scriptures that others have truncated to pithy sayings that were not matching the message. Unfortunately, this happens all too often on Sunday mornings or other gatherings and often loaded with virtue signals.

I set out to understand, read, and yet, it became apparent that Spiritu Ambulatio is so foundational that it should be a Sola! I didn't know that this would end up being my discovery.

And the result is that the message is simply that God loves us all. Many of us don't fit in the middle of the distribution curve. We are often outliers with amazing gifts that our leaders seem to want to squeeze into their boundary marker of the "normal Christian with no variation." After reading these passages over and over, there's no conclusion other than God is up to something and He wants us to join him.

Thanks for picking up this book. It's a long process I'm asking you to take on. I am therefore uploading a few electronic files that you may choose to use if you wish. I'm creating a website for this discussion. Please visit. I am very interested in what the response will be. I will create space for you to share what you experience as you go. It's under development at www.6thsola.com.

Press On

This book is my way of putting a stake in the ground and explaining what I mean by Sola Spiritu Ambulatio. And I say, let's end the Reformation and go forward in transformation. This brings me back to Paul's words in Philippians.

> Philippians 3:12–16
>
> [12] _Not_ that I have _already_ obtained *it* or have already _become perfect_, but _I press on_ so that I may lay hold of that for which also I was laid hold of by Christ Jesus. [13] Brethren, I do not regard myself as having laid hold of *it* yet; but one thing *I do*: _forgetting what lies behind_ and reaching forward to _what lies ahead_, [14] I press on toward the goal for _the prize of the upward call of God_ in Christ Jesus. [15] Let us therefore, as many as are perfect, _have this attitude_; and if in anything you have a _different attitude_, God will reveal that also to you; [16] however, let us _keep living_ by that same _standard_ to which we have attained.

And the standard is the Galatian's freedom, a mindset, an attitude of walking in the Spirit and delivering the fruit of the Spirit in all our relationships. That's the process.

CHAPTER 11

TRANSFORM THE WORLD, ONE PERSON AT A TIME

From the iconic 1997 Apple commercial narrated by Steve Jobs,

Here's to the crazy ones, the misfits, the rebels. The troublemakers, the round pegs in the square holes. The ones who see things differently.

They're not fond of rules and they have no respect for the status quo. You can quote them, disagree with them, glorify or vilify them. About the only thing you can't do is ignore them...because they change things, they push the human race forward.

While some may see them as "the crazy ones," we see genius. Because the people who are crazy enough to think they can change the world—are the ones who do.

Yes, I Am A Crazy One

As with the Five Solas, forming a foundation of understanding of faith, the Sixth Sola is now set to change the world. I may only walk my path, my calling, and seek to be transformed by the Spirit. The results are the fruit, how much love, joy, peace, patience, kindness, goodness, faithfulness, gentleness, and self-control may pour forth from my moment-by-moment living. That is all I have control over. And even "control" is not exactly true. Our foundations of faith are filled with our natural man.

We have been sold a religion of striving for the middle, the perfection, the center of the distribution curve. Eliminating variation, we become a harmonious community where we are all Stepford wives of the faith.

That is the question. Is there any other way to live? The continuous debates we have about who is right theologically has driven us back to searching the Scriptures to be "right" and not to have this transformation to what we often call, "being like Jesus" and using expressions like, "What Would Jesus Do?" My call is to Spiritu Ambulatio living, starting with the Great Relationship, the last words from Jesus to His disciples as recorded by the last Gospel, from the beloved disciple. He's the one we may start with, the "What Is That To You? You Follow Me!" or WITTY? YFM! living.

We have been living over 500 years with a "group" reformation mentality that has been our priority over our own walk and our own transformation. There are many activities that those with a voice may virtue signal to the followers of Christ. They are exemplified in the effort to reach the world with the gospel, especially unreached groups, and yet the message from the Scriptures is that of a living God. A Holy Spirit that will lead His followers as they walk in the Spirit.

Leaders, Think Coaching Not Only Teaching

The drive to Reformation and improved leadership structures is more and more organizational tweaking. And yet, I make the case that we are all to transform, we know this. We are familiar with Romans 12 and the message about renewing our minds. Yet we so easily are influenced to join a "vision caster." I am saying the Holy Spirit is your "vision caster," follow him.

We are sent messages daily to join the effort, and we may be called to service that looks like traditional missionary work, yet I ask that we remind ourselves and others that we serve not from the influence of other humans, but a deep relationship with God. The Great Relationship. That's how the power of the Holy Spirit brings us to our place of service.

Go ahead and question your leadership and their desire to protect the flock. Martin Luther was not perfect, and yet he influenced a departure from the organized religion of his day. There were others that entered the debate from all sides. The splintering effect of Reformation was present at the very early stages and continues to this day. I am reminded of Thomas Müntzer, who began as a supporter of Martin Luther only to turn against him a few years later. There were others who went their own way as well.

Not often preached, nor asked based on Paul's comments in Philippians 2:19–26.

> [19] But _I hope_ in the Lord Jesus to _send Timothy_ to you shortly, so that I also may be encouraged when I learn of your condition. [20] For _I have no one else of kindred spirit_ who will genuinely be concerned for your welfare. [21] For _they all seek after their own interests_, not those of Christ Jesus. [22] But you know of his proven worth, that he served with me in the furtherance of the gospel like a child *serving* his father. [23] Therefore _I hope to send him immediately_, as soon as I see how things *go* with me; [24] and I trust in the Lord that I myself also will be coming shortly. [25] _But_ I thought it necessary _to send to you Epaphroditus_, my brother and fellow worker and fellow soldier, who is also your messenger and minister to my need; [26] because he was longing for you all and was distressed because you had heard that he was sick.

Paul wants to send Timothy and he states that he has "no one else" and that the others "seek after their own interests." But then Paul immediately says that he's sending Epaphroditus.

Let's ask a few questions about what Paul was communicating. Imagine Epaphroditus delivering this letter to the Philippians. They read about how wonderful Timothy was, and that all others are seeking after their own interests. And there stands Epaphroditus delivering the letter.

Would the Philippian leaders reading this break out in laughter? They might look Epaphroditus in the eye and ask him, "So what is the interest that you seek?" Now perhaps this view is an outlier thought. However, for me, it raises the question about sitting at the feet of others. Is this pastor truly looking out for others' interests or their own? There are those that debate that female preachers/prophetesses should have no authority over a man, but what man should have authority? A man that went to seminary and has a piece of paper? A man like Timothy, maybe, but are there any of those?

Get In The Gym

This is my call to read, to go to the Spiritual gym. It's all there for us to be guided by the Holy Spirit in the Word, which is often the person of the Holy Spirit.

We now have all the resources necessary to be our own Timothy. It is best practice to be in fellowship with others pursing the Spiritu Ambulatio, the walking in the Spirit. Yet having a human shepherd is not our calling. Our calling is to hear the "What Is That To You?" question and listen to the "You Follow Me!" John wrote it, we have no need of teachers, yet we are drawn to them as it is the proper path. But in the end, you are the hero. The Holy Spirit is ready to be your guide. It is not about me or anyone else teaching you. Here's a reminder from the beloved disciple John (1 John 2:26–27):

> ²⁶ These things I have written to you concerning those who are trying _to deceive you_. ²⁷ As for you, the _anointing_ which you received from Him _abides in you_, and you have _no need for anyone to teach you_; but as His _anointing teaches_ you about all things, and is true and is not a lie, and just as it has taught you, you abide in Him.

There are those attempting to deceive us. There are spiritual battles when our enemy attempts to influence us, and yet John confidently says, "you have no need for anyone to teach you."

The call to action is for us all to walk in the Spirit. And if you are able to encourage others to pursue their calling, their transformation, and willing to do that moment by moment, please do so. If, however, this sounds intangible, I ask that you take up the challenge to follow the Holy Spirit's work through the Scriptures. This book is for the many Christians. You respect the Word, so read it with the intent to see if there is more Holy Spirit than you may have thought. The current format of our Bibles has made the "rollout" of the church a bit confusing. I suspect the order was not well thought-out, and it's not for me to debate it. Today, we have electronics and it is relatively easy to put these books in the near order of their writing.

Recall that I was not that interested in anything other than Paul. And yet, at that point, 130 chapters, I added Peter, James, John, and Jude. Peter brings out another aspect of what was happening. He wasn't as "stellar" of a disciple when we see his denial, restoration, his desire to be better than John. His attachment to being a Jew and his preference for tradition led to Paul rebuking him to his face.

Peter backs off the enthusiasm and sticks with the Jewish people. He was fine with sending Paul out to the Gentiles, and yet we see a consistent statement between Paul and Peter, and even an acknowledgement that Peter respected Paul even in his embarrassing encounters. These are men with flesh, remember that as we read.

In Peter's last writing in our Scriptures, 2 Peter 1, he begins.

¹ Simon Peter, a bond-servant and apostle of Jesus Christ,

To those who have received a faith of *the same kind as ours*, by the righteousness of our God and Savior, Jesus Christ: ² *Grace* and *peace* be multiplied to you in the knowledge of God and of Jesus our Lord; ³ seeing that His divine power has granted to us everything pertaining to life and godliness, through the true knowledge of *Him who called us* by His own glory and excellence.⁴ For by these He has granted to us *His precious* and *magnificent promises*, so that by them you may become partakers of *the* divine nature, having *escaped the corruption* that is in the world by lust. ⁵ *Now for this very reason* also, *applying all diligence*, in your faith supply *moral excellence*, and in *your* moral excellence, *knowledge*, ⁶ and in *your* knowledge, *self-control*, and in *your* self-control, *perseverance*, and in *your* perseverance, *godliness*, ⁷ and in *your* godliness, *brotherly kindness*, and in *your* brotherly kindness, *love*. ⁸ For if *these qualities* are yours and are *increasing*, they render you neither useless *nor unfruitful* in the true knowledge of our Lord Jesus Christ. ⁹ For he who lacks these *qualities* is blind *or* short-sighted, having *forgotten his purification from his former sins*. ¹⁰ Therefore, brethren, be all the *more diligent* to make certain about *His calling and choosing you;* for as long as you practice these things, you will never stumble; ¹¹ for in this way the entrance into the eternal kingdom of our Lord and Savior Jesus Christ will be *abundantly supplied to you*.

¹² *Therefore*, I will always be ready to *remind you* of these things, even *though you already know them*, and have been established in the truth which is present with *you*. ¹³ I

consider it right, as long as I am in this *earthly* dwelling, to *stir you up by way of reminder*, ¹⁴ knowing that *the laying aside* of my *earthly* dwelling is imminent, as also our Lord Jesus Christ has made clear to me. ¹⁵ And I will also *be diligent* that at any time after my departure you will be able to *call these things to mind*.

¹⁶ For *we did not* follow *cleverly devised tales* when we made known to you *the power and coming of our Lord Jesus Christ*, but *we were eyewitnesses* of His majesty. ¹⁷ For when He received honor and glory from God the Father, such an utterance as this was made to Him by the Majestic Glory, "*This is My beloved Son with whom I am well-pleased*"— ¹⁸ and *we ourselves heard* this utterance made from heaven when we were with Him on the holy mountain.

¹⁹ *So* we have *the prophetic word made* more sure, to which you do well to *pay attention* as to a lamp shining in a dark place, until the day dawns and the morning star arises in your hearts. ²⁰ But know this first of all, that *no prophecy of Scripture* is *a matter of one's own interpretation*, ²¹ for no prophecy was *ever made by an act of human will*, but *men moved by the Holy Spirit spoke from God*.

Remember the context: Peter is at the end of his life. He was blessed with being called a disciple and we read of his relationship with Jesus. He was with him, he walked on water, he was truly as he says here, an eyewitness. He heard God speak from heaven. Yet, he also denied him during the final days, and then after being restored, was even foolishly rebuked. John provided that insight.

Here Peter discusses the "increasing qualities."

⁵ Now for this very reason also,
applying all diligence, in your faith
<u>*supply*</u>
<u>*moral excellence*</u>*, and in your moral excellence,*
<u>*knowledge*</u>*, ⁶ and in your knowledge,*
<u>*self-control*</u>*, and in your self-control,*
<u>*perseverance*</u>*, and in your perseverance,*
<u>*godliness*</u>*, ⁷ and in your godliness,*
<u>*brotherly kindness*</u>*, and in your brotherly kindness,*
<u>*love*</u>*. ⁸*

For if
<u>*these qualities*</u> *are yours and are*
<u>*increasing*</u>

Let's Get Better

These are similar to the fruit of the Spirit, yet they are not exactly the same. Peter provides a graceful view of how we are to evaluate ourselves. Carl Friedrich Gauß has the curve for it. Let's move from below average on these qualities and increase. That's the message from the Sola Spiritu Ambulatio.

Give grace to others, listen to others, and be diligent with your time to prepare your mind for renewal and transformation. This is my offering to the body of Christ. Let's walk in the Spirit. I don't have this all figured out, but what I do is continue to remind myself that we have a living God and we have this mysterious Holy Spirit. I need this word and the Holy Spirit to allow me to show up each day to be a blessing to others.

We all have our paths, our histories, our experiences. Let's take ownership of our spiritual exercises, lifting the weights, building the muscle. My intention is to bring coaching to help you increase confidence in your Great Relationship.

May you find your calling and confidently step out with the power of the Holy Spirit. And may your confidence grow by reading from the source.

The Sixth Sola, walking in the Spirit—a choice we make now more than ever, and let it be our reminder in how to move forward. The forest, the big picture, is our living God working today. Martin Luther didn't have the internet, but we do, and I offer you to visit with me at www.6thsola.com. I have tools that will help jump-start your own reading program.

I wish to hear from you, the reader. The "revival" starts with the living God, and His Holy Spirit, and we can prepare by transforming and walking in the Spirit, the Spiritu Ambulatio. Do you want to change the world? Let's start with ourselves. I'm in.

It's up to you to take action,

1. To simply walk in the Spirit, and if that's not understood, then
2. Make a commitment to read the post-Resurrection words in 22 weeks, one chapter at a time, and record your thoughts. God has given you a body, soul, mind, and spirit.

You are the hero every day. The Holy Spirit has always been offering to be our guide. You have a calling, you have purpose, and it may not stay the same, it may change. Embrace that change that God has gifted you, and you will be empowered to do your calling.

We are done with Reformation. You transform, I transform, and we serve with fruit and our gifts. I wish you the best in building confidence in God's presence and the power that He provides through His Holy Spirit.

Grace, mercy, and peace.

www.ingramcontent.com/pod-product-compliance
Lightning Source LLC
Chambersburg PA
CBHW071200070526
44584CB00019B/2862